Italian Khana

Photographs
Sephi Bergerson

RANDOM HOUSE INDIA

Published by Random House India in 2008
13579108642

Random House Publishers India Private Limited
301 World Trade Tower, Barakhamba Lane
New Delhi 110001
contact@randomhouse.co.in
www.randomhouse.co.in

Random House Group Limited
20 Vauxhall Bridge Road
London SW1V 2SA
United Kingdom

ISBN 978 81 8400 021 4

Printed and bound in India by Ajanta Offset

For my love, who always took the 'funny cook' seriously

Contents

Introduction

Introduction

There are very few countries where everything stops for a midday meal. The land of Italy is among these. At noon, the streets fall silent in every town. From inside the houses drift distant sounds: the clinking of glasses, laughter and raised voices. In Italy, meals are never simply about eating. They are important social occasions which can stretch for hours, an opportunity for families and friends to come together to catch up on gossip and the day's news, for jokes, arguments and table thumping. Italians love celebration and they love to eat, so every meal becomes a celebration. It is a wonderful way to live.

Indians have a particular affinity for Italian food. I recently read Gregory David Robert's *Shantaram,* in which he says that Indians are the Italians of Asia, and every Italian has a bit of Indian in him. I could not agree more. The importance of meals in Italian culture, the passion thrown into cooking them, the treasuring of granny's or mommy's special recipes which the wife can never make in quite the same way, the arguments over whether the cooking is finer in Tuscany or Sicily, the big, hospitable smiles, the family ties. All of it is so familiar to us.

I remember my amazement when I had my first taste of slightly bitter marzipan in Regaleali, in Sicily about 15 years ago. It was so much like our own badam barfi. And the crispy, salty panelle, again from Sicily—just like our own bhujia. And the time when I was taken to a trattoria in Sarzana, a town in Liguria, for farinata di ceci, which was nothing but our very own besan pooda. It would be wrong to say that Italian and Indian food are very similar in taste, but there is something about both cuisines which is able to fill that hole in our stomach. It's the simplicity of the Italian kitchen, its warmth and heartiness that really connects with our taste buds. That's why most Indians, craving for some desi khana after a week in Europe, tend to run for some pizza or a penne arrabiata.

So what is food in Italy all about? Huge plates of fettuccini Alfredo? Coleslaw? Pan-fried pizzas? Heavens, no! It is slices of ciabatta drenched in olive oil—not pomace, but the real thing. It is fine, translucent slivers of Parma ham sliced off the bone, with just the right amount of pungency and smokiness. It is a steaming bowl of durum wheat spaghetti accompanied with a sauce of ripe, sweet tomatoes, their bite still intact, and garden-fresh basil. It is a wedge of mild Gorgonzola cheese and a bunch of ready-to-burst grapes.

Carefully prepared, strikingly simple, with flawless ingredients, that's what food in Italy is all about.

Italian food is all about its splendid land and its splendid people. It is about food markets which are alive with the freshest produce, ready to be lovingly prepared for the family. And the food is as varied as the landscape. Dishes like lightly fried squid and clams give off the aroma of the sea, and lamb stew cooked over a slow fire tastes of the earth. Italy's flavourful tomatoes, miles upon miles of them vying for the southern sun, taste, indeed, of the sun. Carefully prepared, strikingly simple, with flawless ingredients, that's what food in Italy is all about. And that's why it is the world's most popular cuisine.

My love affair with Italian food began when I was sixteen. I had dropped out of school and was travelling all over Italy, trying to sell marble. Everywhere I went, I was surrounded by food. Markets overflowed with boisterously coloured fruits and vegetables. In small shops I found baskets of still warm ricotta cheese. I could hear the hiss and sizzle of artichokes dropped in hot oil in the Jewish quarters in Rome. If I close my eyes I can still smell them.

Here I have to thank my dear friend Serra, with whom I discovered the joys of Italian food. We took many trips around the country together in search of a perfect meal. Oh! The red mullet encrusted with black olive pâté, with just a squeeze of lemon, at Enoteca Pinchiorri in Florence; the buttery goose liver which just melts in your mouth at Locanda Dell'Angelo in Sarzana; my first sip of Tignanello, one of Italy's most special wines; the peculiar whiff of truffles that appeared strange to my as yet unexposed palate.

I was impressed by the regional diversity and quirky recipes, each with an even quirkier story behind it. I learnt to respect the importance of meals, which were announced when the woman of the house put the pasta in the water. This was the point when bread was laid out, wine was poured and everyone had to take their seats. It was a great offence to let the pasta wait on the table for you. For me, the best meals were at Serra's home, where the conversation at dinner was always about the menu for the following day's lunch. Her mother made the best zucchini and feta cheese fritters in the world, and her food has always featured in some way on all my menus.

My Italian love affair quickly turned into full-blown obsession and a few years later, I did a professional about-turn and opened MezzaLuna, a chic little Italian restaurant, in Delhi.

I always say I am a fake chef, for with Italian food, what's most important really, is quality ingredients.

Passion has no reason, but if I had to explain why it was Italian cuisine that caught my attention and not French or Spanish or Moroccan, here it is. At the end of the day, it is the simplicity of the cooking which has always drawn me to Italian cuisine. I always say I am a fake chef, for with Italian food, what's most important really, is quality ingredients. The methods and techniques are so easy. After running an Indian restaurant for many years (Vama, my successful Indian restaurant in London, which I opened after MezzaLuna failed, but more on that later), the lazy chef in me opted for cooking Italian.

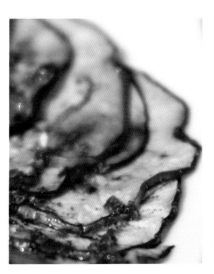

I never went to a catering school, nor do I have any formal training. I cannot chop at the speed of lightning like trained chefs, nor do I know how to stick a thermometer into a roast to see if the meat is done. I learnt to cook while eating with friends and travelling, and I have never felt anything was amiss in this. Even when I have friends coming home, I prefer to cook Italian, not only because I am expected to but also because compared to Indian cooking, it is so much simpler, so much quicker, and yes, sometimes so much more impressive.

You don't need fancy or unusual equipment. Nor do you need any particular expertise or specialised cooking knowledge.

And that's why I've written this book, because I think it's time every Indian home learnt to rustle up some delicious and authentic Italian food effortlessly. We're eating more and more of it at restaurants (my restaurant Diva runs to a full house most evenings and the people who come in are usually regulars), yet at Diva we serve food that's meant to be cooked at home, to eat with family and friends, and the best possible cuisine to entertain with—low on effort, high on impact. And don't let the foreign ingredients scare you. As I will show you, it is possible to adapt the ingredients without messing around with their authenticity. You don't need fancy or unusual equipment. Nor do you need any particular expertise or specialised cooking knowledge. A fire, a pan, a little imagination, a lot of enthusiasm and wonderful music in the background and you will be able to cook not just a good, but a great Italian meal.

The recipes in the pages to come are simple to cook, which does not mean that they lack sophistication or imagination. Each recipe represents what I value the most. Ingredients which are fresh and easy to find, and, most important, methods which will not intimidate you. I have tried to preserve the honesty and individuality of each recipe, but modified them where necessary, keeping in mind what is available in India's markets, and what is not.

I will start with basic recipes which will inspire you and build your confidence to take the next steps—an intimate supper for your lover, or a fancy dinner party, maybe even a meal to impress your mother-in-law (a tall order!).

This book is not organised the way Italian cookbooks usually are, following the traditional pattern of courses in an Italian meal—appetisers (antipasti), pasta, fish (pesce), meat (carne) and dessert (dolce). I have instead organised the recipes according to the occasion and the moods in which you will cook. Towards the end of the book I have suggested menus which I hope you will find useful.

In Italy, the order in which you add the ingredients and their quantities are never really respected. You learn to cook by observing rather than following recipes. Sometimes steps are skipped and ingredients are forgotten. Very often recipes are modified, or another ingredient is added, so much so, that after a while no one really knows what the original recipe was. You will find many such recipes in the 'Cooking with friends' chapter. These recipes, then, are really a starting point, to get your creative juices flowing rather than set out a rigid path to be followed religiously. I have tried to preserve this flavour of Italian cooking, to guide you the way I was taught, with instructions like 'generous dash of olive oil', 'plenty of grated Parmesan' and 'cook till soft'. I promise, you will do just fine with these.

I hope the recipes in this book give you pleasure and a sense of Italian food. Most of all I hope they inspire you to eat the Italian way—with much joy, with loved ones around you, and always with a dash of celebration.

Food map of Italy

Fontina cheese
Grappa
Petti di pollo alla
valdostana

Gorgonzola , Mascarpone
& Grana Padano cheeses
Salami milano—most
famous Italian sausage
Polenta alla griglia

Gnocchi
Tagliatelle with four
cheeses & sausages

Pinot Grigio wines
Prosciutto di San Danielle—
best Italian cured ham

Trentino-
Alto Adige

Friuli-Venezia Giulia

Valle d'Aosta

Lombardy

Veneto

Piedmont

Asiago cheese
Amarone, Soave &
Valpolicella wines
Prosecco
Polenta
Risi e bisi
Pesce in saor

Balsamic vinegar from
Modena
Parmesan cheese
Parma ham & mortadella
Chicken with balsamic
Spaghetti Bolognese

Emilia Romagna

White truffles
Porcini mushrooms
Robiola & Tomino
cheeses
Barolo &
Barbaresco wines
Bagna cauda
Pana cotta

Liguria

Best olive oil
Sweetest basil
Pesto Genovese
Lobster salad

Toscana

Marche

Amazing restaurants,
among them La vechia
Cartiera in Fabriano,
and Mauro Uliassi

Pecorino cheese
Maiale ai capperi

Umbria

Scamorza cheese
Montepulciano d'abruzzo wine

Stuffed pastas
Crespelle
Chicken mould with
saffron sauce
Torta della nonna

Lazio
• Rome

Abruzzo

Molise

Best olive oil
in the country

Bruschetta
Panzanella
Pasta carbonara
Saltimbocca

Campania

Puglia

Amazing seafood
Famous fish roe
called bottarga
Vernaccia di Oristano
& Cannonau wines

Sardinia

Mozzarella di bufala, Ricotta
& Mascarpone cheeses
Birth place of pizza (Naples)
Insalata caprese
Melanzane alla Parmigiana

Basilicata

Calabria

Best sun dried tomatoes,
blood oranges, prickly pears,
eggplant, olives & capers
Fuoco sauce
Marzipan
Caponata
Torta di ricotta
Canolli

Sicily

Chillies
Penne arrabiata

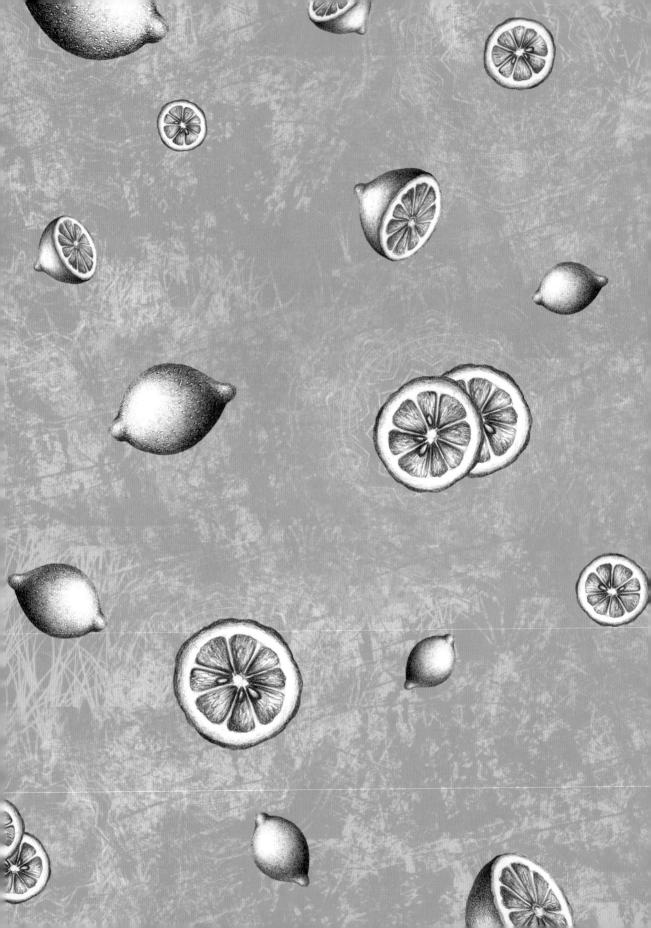

Ingredients of the
Italian kitchen

Ingredients of the
Italian kitchen

Here is a brief introduction to the common ingredients of the Italian kitchen, with tips and techniques on how to cook them. Do please read this section before you start on the recipes.

Pasta

For a list of local suppliers who should be able to meet your Italian ingredients needs, see the list I have provided at the end of the book (p 218).

Pasta sums up the essence and soul of the Italian kitchen. It is an essential part of every Italian meal, and is rarely a meal by itself. Pasta transcends all boundaries in Italy. The poor as well as the rich, from north to south, passionately eat it. There is no end to how many shapes and varieties of pasta there are, but here we'll just stick to some classics. Today almost every sort of pasta is easily available in India—you even have a choice of brands.

The most common pastas available in India's metros are:
- **penne rigate**, tube shaped
- **farfalle**, literally means butterfly, and looks like a bow
- **fusilli**, spiral shaped
- **conchiglie**, literally means conch shell; they look like ridged, slightly oval shaped bowls
- **spaghetti**
- **linguine**, a thinner and flatter version of spaghetti
- **angel hair**, long, extremely thin strands
- **tagliatelle**, slightly wider, flatter strands of spaghetti
- **tagliolini**, thinner version of tagliatelle and contains egg
- **lasagna sheets**, wide, flat sheets of pasta

When choosing a pasta shape for a sauce, there are no hard and fast rules, but I always prefer to use thin pastas like spaghetti and tagliolini for olive oil-based or delicate sea-food sauces. Short pastas like penne or conchiglie are good for chunkier, meatier sauces, as the broad openings and ridges in these pasta are ideal to trap the sauce. Always buy dried pasta made from durum wheat. It stays very well for weeks in an airtight container.

Then there is stuffed pasta, which you make with fresh pasta dough and fresh stuffings, such as ravioli, which are like little pillows, or cappelletti, literally meaning cap of the pope. I have not listed any recipes with filled fresh, homemade pasta because it is too time consuming and you need some specialised tools to make these. You are better off enjoying them at Diva!

Cooking pasta is easy, fun and quick as long as one keeps a few simple rules in mind.

- Pasta must always be cooked in an abundance of boiling water, salt and olive oil. Not everyone would agree with me about the olive oil part, especially southern Italians, but I find a dash of olive oil in boiling water always ensures that the pasta does not get sticky.

- Now comes the tricky part—the cooking time. The only true gauge is your own sense of when the pasta is ready, backed up by repeated testing. When the pasta is al dente (firm at the centre, yet tender), it is ready to be drained and sauced. Look at the directions on your pasta packet and follow the cooking time specified for each shape and type of pasta. For example, penne will take a couple of minutes longer than spaghetti. If you want al dente pasta, in true Italian manner, then cook the pasta a minute less than the time specified on the packet, as it will cook again with the sauce.

- I personally like to add a lump of butter or olive oil to the pasta before the sauce is added. This helps to enrich the final flavor.

- Pasta should ideally be served in a shallow soup plate. Flat plates cause the pasta to cool off too quickly, and have no edge against which to brace your fork for twirling. If you don't have a shallow soup plate, use a flat plate with a rim.

- Cheese is not always served with pasta, although it is a frequent accompaniment. Seafood sauces are never served with cheese! Taste the pasta first to see if you think it needs cheese. Do not automatically blanket the pasta with Parmesan. It should be an accent, not the main taste. In southern Italy, dried toasted bread crumbs are used to top pasta with absolutely delicious results.

If you like to cook pasta frequently, a well-stocked pantry will provide a limitless variety of pasta dishes at literally a moment's notice. A few basics are extra virgin olive oil, Parmesan, dry oregano, fresh basil, parsley, lemon, chilli flakes, garlic and fresh tomatoes. And of course, eternal wine, both red and white.

Last, but not least, I always like to make a sauce which will be done by the time the pasta is boiled, so that the flavours remain fresh.

Risotto

Rice plays almost as important a role as pasta in Italian kitchens, mainly as a primo, or the first course. The risotto is like the Italian khichdi. Said to have been invented in Milan, it is made with superfine rice such as Arborio and Carnaroli. Cooking risotto is quite different to our Indian ways of cooking rice. When cooking it, the most important thing you need is patience. For me, it is always a stress-buster. That 20 minutes of slowly stirring the rice is, in a way, like ironing clothes—somewhat mindless, and very relaxing!

All risotto is prepared the same way, where rice is coated in butter or oil, then hot stock (which has been simmering on the stove) is added to it, a ladle at a time (about half a cup), and the rice is stirred over a low heat. Only once all the liquid has been absorbed is more stock added. Always make sure there is enough liquid to cook the rice; it should bubble gently like old-fashioned oatmeal or what we call daliya. The process continues till the rice is tender and creamy, but still retains a 'bite'—approximately 20 minutes.

The final touch, and the most important technique for making risotto, is called mantecatura, which literally means off the heat. At this point, a dash of butter or spoonful of olive oil is added to the cooked risotto, which is then covered for a couple of minutes. This makes the risotto creamy and gives it a pleasing glaze.

Shellfish

Whatever the size, all types of prawns and shrimps can be cooked in salted boiling water until they turn pink, and then can be used in various ways—in a sauce for pasta, rubbed with salt and lemon and grilled over hot coals, pan-fried, or just boiled and served with mayonnaise. Always shell prawns after cooking as this helps retain maximum flavour. But don't forget to de-vein them before cooking. Pull off the head and pull out the black, thread-like intestine (you will see the black thread as soon as you make a slit on the back of the prawn) with the tip of a knife, and wash the prawns under running water.

Fish

Fish plays a very important role on an Italian table, thanks to Italy's extensive coastline. Italians like their fish to be cooked very simply, usually grilled or baked, with olive oil and lemon. Fish soup is found in every coastal area, each region having its own version, and each claiming that theirs is the best.

Whole fish needs to be gutted, which means the insides need to be removed, before cooking. Gutting involves removing the fin, guts and kidney line, and is really not the most pleasant task. Thankfully you can always get your fishmonger to do it for you. If you are pan-frying or grilling the fish, the scales should also be removed with a blunt knife, working from the tail towards the head. In case you plan to bake or poach the fish, leave the scales on as they will hold the fish together. All my fish recipes are made for fillets but you can use them to cook whole fish if you want, as this does look more impressive when served.

I have always substituted our local fish for the ones specified in Italian recipes. Easily available fish are red snapper, bekti, pomfret, sole, singur, king fish, sea bass and mackerel, just to name a few. There's no reason why you can't substitute your local fish, or fish of your choice for the one mentioned in the recipe.

Meat

Though veal is the favoured meat of Italians, the Italian kitchen also uses a lot of poultry, lamb and pork. We are going to restrict ourselves to lamb, chicken and pork, since they are most easily available to us.

Mutton dressed as lamb

In most parts of India, mutton, and not lamb, predominates. Mutton cooks very differently from lamb. It absorbs flavours more readily but isn't suitable for quick cooking techniques such as grilling or pan frying as the meat gets tough and dry. I am not ashamed to admit I have been using milk or raw papaya as a tenderiser for mutton, pork and duck, and have found that it doesn't interfere with the flavour of the meat at all. I particularly recommend tenderising mutton with grated papaya, a technique that is familiar to Indian cooking. Cover the meat with grated, raw papaya for at least an hour. Then take it out of the marinade and wash and dry it before starting to cook.

The basic cuts of meat used in Italian cooking are the tender parts, such as chops or loin, which are best grilled or pan-fried. The tougher parts, such as shoulder and breast, are best braised or slow cooked in the oven. The two cuts that I have used in this book are chops (chaampe) and cubes (tikka), both easily available with our Indian butchers. I have used minced meat (kheema) in a couple of recipes, which again is easily available. You don't need to marinate this.

When using chops, ask the butcher to make one chop out of three ribs. That way you will get a nice chunky piece of meat rather than a tiny piece hanging from a bone.

Pork

We have fairly good quality pork available to us in India although it is still harder to find than mutton. It is worth getting hold of for special occasions. I like to use chops from the ribs and loin (from the back portion of the pig) for my recipes, as they cook fairly quickly. Pork braised in milk is a great delicacy, and normally Italians like to roast it with sage or rosemary. Thankfully, now there are many reliable pork suppliers in most of our cities, and gone are the days when we needed to be the adventurous sort to cook pork.

You should still take care not to source your pork from a dodgy supplier because you could get very sick if the meat has not been cleaned and processed properly. Many companies which earlier just exported pork products, such as Meatzza, have started retailing bacon, sausages and other processed pork products now. All Oberoi hotels also retail reasonably priced pork products, processed in-house. For a list of good pork suppliers see p 218.

Chicken

Italians don't often use chicken pieces as we do in our dishes. I have used chicken breast in most of my recipes as it is both healthier and easier to store, but stews and classic poultry recipes call for whole chickens. Here I leave the choice to you. Use whatever is convenient.

Vegetables

I was born a vegetarian. The reason why I was exposed to Italian food at an early age was because when we would travel, Italian was the only cuisine which offered us poor vegetarians some options, unlike other European kitchens where the concept of vegetarianism just did not exist. In fact, in the south of Italy, where meat is a luxury, vegetables are quite often seen at the table as a dish in their own right.

There are no special tips for cooking vegetables the Italian way. The only advice I would add is to use the freshest vegetables, and cook what is in season. Don't overcook the vegetables—you should be able to taste and feel the texture. Most of the recipes call for vegetables which are easily available to us such as carrots, beans, cauliflower, tomatoes, peppers, onions and garlic. Some like zucchini, asparagus and leeks, termed 'English vegetables' in India, are also grown locally, and you can buy them fresh in most of our cities.

Lime versus lemon

In India we don't generally get the lemons that Italians use, but lime (nimboo). Lemon has a thicker waxier skin, and the juice is not as strong and sharp as our lime juice. If I can't find lemons I just substitute lime, for the only thing one needs to do is reduce the quantity of juice called for by the recipe. I have written all my recipes based on lime juice, so should you find real lemons and wish to use them, just increase the quantity of juice a bit.

Where you need to use the zest (peel) of lemon or orange, do so taking care to leave out the bitter white pith. I normally substitute lemon zest with sweet lime (mausambi) peel or orange peel, and it works quite well.

Cheese

What would life be if there were no Parmesan to grate over pasta, or a pizza without mozzarella? Fortunately, more or less all the basic Italian cheeses are now available in India's big cities, plus many of the specialty Italian cheeses are available in select outlets. You cannot substitute processed cheese for any of the cheeses specified in my recipes. Flanders Dairy makes wonderful mozzarella, goat's cheese, ricotta and mascarpone, and they have an outlet in every city, so don't even think of taking out your tub of Amul or Kraft.

Parmigiano Reggiano

Better known as Parmesan, this one is really the king of Italian cheeses. A hard granular cheese, it is not to be confused with American Parmesan, which is totally different. You can nibble on a piece of Parmesan with a glass of wine, grate it over your pasta, and eat yet another piece with marmalade as dessert. You could make a full meal out of it! There are many brands available in India. The ones I prefer are Zanetti and Galbani, both available in all Indian metros.

Mascarpone

A heavier version of cream cheese, it is used very often in pasta sauces, and desserts. In fact it is the key ingredient in tiramisu. Flanders Dairy now produces mascarpone in India, so in case you can't get hold of Italian mascarpone (also available), you could use the locally made one.

Gorgonzola

This is my all-time favourite blue-veined cheese from Lombardy, and you can see from the recipes that I am a bit partial to it. It too can be eaten on its own, makes wonderful sauces, and stands proudly on a cheese platter. There is no local substitute for it, and if you do not find Gorgonzola, choose another recipe.

Ricotta

This grainy cheese resembles chhena or crumbled paneer, but is much lighter since it is made of sheep's milk. However, I don't recommend you substitute cottage cheese or paneer for it as the taste is totally different, and you won't need to do so anyway as ricotta too is produced locally, in addition to Italian imports available in all the metros. Ricotta is used in desserts, pasta and for antipasti. My favourite way of eating it is as a dessert, with a spoonful of honey drizzled over it.

The Italian
bhandar

The Italian bhandar

Here is a list of store items that I suggest you have handy while using this book, and if you decide you quite like the idea of cooking Italian regularly. A well-stocked cupboard and fridge will not only save you time, you'll also be able to prepare a stupendous meal at a moment's notice.

You will be able to find all these items in any good store in your city. For a list of specialty products suppliers in the four metros, see p 218. I have also described some of the more foreign ingredients listed below.

Store cupboard

Seasonings

- **Black peppercorns**, whole in a pepper mill. If the pepper is ground beforehand it loses its oomph and aroma. There's nothing to beat having a good pepper mill handy, which you can adjust according to how coarse or fine you want the pepper to be. You could also consider crushing your peppercorn by hand, in a pestle and mortar where you will get an even coarser ground pepper.
- **Dried red chillies**
- **Bay leaves**—our good old tej patta
- **Fennel seeds**—saunf
- **Nutmeg**, whole, and to be grated on the spot when required as a seasoning
- **Cinnamon**, powdered
- **Cloves**
- **Dried oregano**
- **Salt**: I prefer to use coarse Maldon sea salt but that is not easily available. Catch's free flowing salt works perfectly as well.

Cans, bottles & jars

- **Tinned tomatoes**: Both whole and pulp. There are many brands available now, however, I find Divella to be among the best.

- **Capers**: Small gray-green flower buds, frequently used in Italian cooking, especially in sharply flavoured sauces.

- **Black and green olives**, plain, not stuffed

- **Olive oil**: Here I am a bit prejudiced, for this is the one ingredient I would not compromise on. Look at the bottle carefully and do not buy pomace, also a type of olive oil but good only for frying and not for cooking. My personal favourite oil is Philipo Berio, but Colavita offers a very good extra virgin oil as well. Extra virgin olive oil is the first result of a cold press and has a very low level of acidity. It is considered the finest, most fruity, and hence, the most expensive variety of olive oil. Pure olive oil, or just plain olive oil, is a blend between extra virgin and refined olive oil. It has a slightly higher level of acidity. Use normal olive oil for cooking and extra virgin olive oil for salads, drizzling and soups.

- **Balsamic vinegar**: King of all vinegars, balsamic has a sweetness and depth which can't be found in any other vinegar. In Indian markets synthetic balsamic is available, which will work, but if you can afford it, go for the 12 year old oak-aged balsamic from Modena, available at select stores in Delhi and Mumbai.

- **White and red wine**: As the cliché goes, I am a firm believer that any wine which is not good enough for drinking is not good enough for cooking with. Thankfully, we now have enough decent wines available in the Indian market, and you should be fine with Sula's Sauvignon Blanc and Satori Merlot. If you are in a mood to splurge, I would recommend a good Pinot Grigio when cooking with white, a Cabernet Sauvignon or a Sangiovese when you need red. You could also use Grover's La Reserva, a very good wine, both for drinking as well as cooking.

- **Dijon mustard**: Very different from the regular mustard, Dijon is light in colour and much stronger in flavour. It has a vinegary flavour with a hint of sweetness and is widely available. You may even find it at your next door kirana shop.

- **Sun-dried tomatoes**: Normally sold dry or bottled in oil, these have a very intense flavour.

- **Gherkins**

- **Pine nuts**

Grains, pulses & pasta

- **Chick peas**

- **Plain flour**

- **Pasta**: Many brands are widely available in India and you will find a packet of basic pasta even in your grocery store next door. However I would recommend Barilla or Divella pastas. If you are in the mood to splurge, go for D'Cecco. Store some spaghetti and a short pasta, of which the most commonly available in grocery stores is penne.

- **Risotto rice**: The best types of this medium grain rice are Arborio and Carnaroli. Basmati cannot be substituted. Recommended brands are Divella and D'Cecco.

Miscellaneous items

- **Dried porcini or shiitake mushrooms**
- **Baking powder**
- **Vanilla extract**
- **Yeast**

Fridge

- **Unsalted butter**

- **Parmesan**

- **Fresh single cream** or Vijaya or Amul cream in tetrapacks

- **Eggs:** Free range eggs are easily available, and Keggs offers fantastic golden yolk eggs.

- **Bacon:** I recommend using a leaner variety unless specified in the recipe. I normally use the bacon from the Oberoi Hotel shop, or pancetta, which is the Italian version of bacon. For a list of shops where you will find good bacon, see p 218.

- **Cooking chocolate:** I recommend using chocolate with high cocoa content, which is a little more expensive, but the quality and intense flavour more than make up for it. Morde is the locally made brand, but imported brands like Calbout, with a higher cocoa content, are easily available as well.

Vegetable basket

- **Red onions:** They are sweeter and more easily available than white onions.

- **Garlic:** Our Indian variety is sharper than the Italian one, so I have adjusted the quantity in my recipes accordingly.

- **Celery:** We get a thinner variety in India, but this doesn't make a difference to taste.

- **Tomatoes:** Indian tomatoes are different from Italian tomatoes, but I'd rather use fresh local tomatoes than canned Italian ones.

- **Mushrooms:** Never wash these as that makes them gooey. They just need to be wiped clean with a dry cloth.

- **Eggplant**

- **Red or yellow bell peppers**

- **Zucchini**

Herbs

These, particularly basil and parsley, play an important role in Italian cooking, and although fresh herbs are available almost everywhere today, growing your own herbs is a great idea. Even two small pots of basil and parsley on your windowsill would work well. After all, there is something so delicious about plucking herbs fresh, just before adding them to the pan. If you can't find any herbs, then substitute them with the dried versions but reduce the quantity, as their taste is stronger.

Pots, pans & other bits

- **Non-stick shallow pan**
- **Large saucepan**
- **Heavy saucepan**—if you don't have one, use a non-stick pan
- **Deep pot** for boiling pasta
- **Cutting board**, wooden or acrylic
- **Sharp kitchen knife**
- **Roasting pans**, preferably non-stick
- **Tongs** for pasta
- **Colander**
- **Four-sided grater**
- **Pepper mill**
- **Pastry brush**
- **Mixing bowls**
- **Baking pans**—round and rectangular
- **Fluted tart mould**
- **Ladles**
- **Ring mould**
- **Lemon zester**
- **Potato peeler**

Basic
recipes

Basic
recipes

Stocks

Some of the recipes in this book will require the use of stocks, which are light broths made of either vegetable, chicken, meat or fish as flavourings, and used in soups, risottos, sauces and stews. Don't be daunted by the idea of making them—stock-making is not intensive work and makes a big difference to the taste of a dish. Once you get into the habit of making them, you won't be able to stop, I promise! And if you have someone who cooks for you, it's very easy to teach them to make it. There are also basic, simple sauces—pesto, béchamel and tomato—that every self-respecting Italian cook should know. They are simple and will be used in a number of recipes in this book.

All recipes in this book serve 4.

Wherever a recipe calls for stock, you can use either cubes or your own homemade stock. Maggi makes chicken stock cubes which are quite good, and I always keep them handy. Once in a while I cheat and use chicken stock instead of meat stock. The taste does differ slightly but this works well when I am short of time and do not have meat stock handy. My only suggestion is not to cheat with fish stock. If the recipe calls for it, make it fresh rather than substituting it with anything else.

In case you have to make a risotto in a hurry and do not have stock handy, feel free to use Maggi chicken stock cubes or even vegetable stock.

All stocks except fish stock can be refrigerated for at least 3 – 4 days, and can be frozen for a couple of months. You can use either ice cube boxes or simple, zipped plastic pouches.

Chicken stock

1 kg chicken bones and
  carcass, chopped
3 cloves garlic, chopped
1 large onion, chopped
½ kg carrot and celery,
  roughly chopped
4 dried bay leaves
3 lt water
Black peppercorns to season
2 handfuls of any mixed
  fresh herbs

1 Place all the ingredients in a deep, heavy pan and bring
  it to a boil.

2 After the first boil, turn the heat down to low and let the
  stock simmer for a couple of hours, skimming off the fat
  and other bits as and when they come to the surface.

3 Let the stock cool, then pass it through a fine sieve.

Meat stock

1 kg lamb, or lamb bones
  and trimmings cut into
  small, rough pieces
3 cloves garlic,
  roughly chopped
1 large onion,
  roughly chopped
½ kg carrot and celery,
  roughly chopped
4 dried bay leaves
3 lt water
Black peppercorns to season
2 handfuls of any mixed
  fresh herbs

1 Preheat oven to 200°C.

2 Roast the meat and bones in a roasting pan in the oven,
  without oil, for about 45 minutes, till brown.

3 Place the browned meat and bone with all the remaining
  ingredients in a deep, heavy pan and bring to a boil. Turn
  the heat down to low and let the stock simmer for a couple
  of hours, skimming off the fat and other bits as necessary.

4 Let the stock cool, then pass it through a fine sieve. When
  cold, skim the fat, if any, which has solidified on the top.

Vegetable stock

1 kg mixed aromatic root
  vegetables like carrots,
  celery and leeks
2 large onions, chopped
2 cloves garlic, chopped
2 handfuls mixed fresh herbs
A few whole black peppercorns
3 lt water

Place all the ingredients in a deep, heavy pan and bring to a boil. After the first boil, turn the heat down to low and let the stock simmer for a couple of hours. Strain the stock and let it cool.

Vegetable stock makes a great base for light soups.

Fish stock

1 kg fish scraps (bones, tail,
  head or bits and bobs)
1 medium onion, chopped
2 dried bay leaves
1 stick celery
A few whole black peppercorns
3 lt water

Follow the chicken stock recipe: throw in all the ingredients in a heavy saucepan and bring to a boil. Lower the heat and simmer for 2 hours. Strain and cool.

I recommend you don't freeze fish stock, and use it within a couple of days of making it.

Béchamel sauce

Used quite a lot in Italian cooking, béchamel is fairly easy to make. All you need to do is take care that no lumps form while cooking.

50 g unsalted butter
75 g flour
400 ml hot milk
½ tsp nutmeg, freshly grated

1 Melt butter in a saucepan until bubbling. Remove from heat and stir in flour with a whisk. Cook over low heat for 4 – 5 minutes, stirring constantly till the mix becomes crumbly in texture.

2 Add half the hot milk and whisk until smooth. Whisking continuously, add the remaining milk and whisk until smooth. Bring to the boil, add nutmeg, lower heat and simmer for 10 minutes.

> No salt has been added because you do not use béchamel by itself, but as a base for pastas or other sauces. In case your sauce turns lumpy, just give it a 1 second whizz in the food processor. Béchamel can be used hot or cold.

Pesto

Pesto is the classic 'crudo', or uncooked sauce. Only fresh, fragrant basil should be used to make it, which is available in plenty, all year round in most cities. Rich, intensely flavoured pesto is always diluted with a little of the pasta cooking water when served. In case you do not have pine nuts handy, you can use walnuts. I have even used almonds when I have been desperate, but the taste differs a bit.

150 g fresh basil,
  stems removed
4 cloves garlic, peeled
50 g pine nuts, toasted
50 ml extra virgin olive oil,
  divided in 2 equal parts
75 g Parmesan, freshly grated
Salt & pepper to taste

1 Place the basil leaves, garlic and pine nuts in a food processor with a steel blade. Process until the basil and garlic are finely chopped.

2 With the machine still running, add half the olive oil in a slow and steady stream. Turn off the processor, and add the Parmesan. Process again till all the cheese is absorbed.

3 Reduce the speed and add the remaining olive oil, again in a slow stream. When the pesto is creamy, season with salt and pepper.

> Pesto is traditionally made with a pestle and mortar. I think this is very romantic and even have a wonderful old stone set for it. But to be honest, I really cannot remember the last time I made pesto manually.

Basic tomato sauce

For me, this recipe is really the backbone of the Italian kitchen. There are many versions of this sauce, and I have listed two of them: the basic tomato sauce, which works very well with pastas, lasagne and chicken; and the deluxe version, which works as a sauce on its own.

1 kg large, ripe, red tomatoes
40 ml extra virgin olive oil
3 cloves garlic, chopped
1 handful fresh basil
1 pinch red chilli flakes
Water, if required
Salt to taste

1 Cut the tomatoes in half, crosswise, and remove most of the seeds, using your fingers to scoop them out. Quarter the tomatoes.

2 Heat the oil in a large pan and add garlic and chilli flakes. As soon as the garlic gives off its pungent aroma and turns opaque, add the tomatoes. Cook over high heat until the tomato begins to thicken. Use a wooden spoon to stir and help break the tomato pulp, adding some water if the sauce becomes too dry. Add the basil, either whole or roughly chopped, and salt.

3 Remove the sauce from the heat and put it through a food processor for just a minute—you do not want a fine purée, but a chunky sauce with bits of tomatoes in it.

Deluxe tomato sauce

This sauce has a more subtle taste and texture, thanks to the sofrito, which is the base of carrot, celery and onion used in many Italian stews and soups. The sofrito adds a depth of taste to a dish, and in this case, takes away the sharpness of tomatoes and adds a bit of sweetness to the sauce. This also takes much longer to prepare than the basic tomato sauce, but then you can always prepare a batch and freeze it.

1 kg large, red, ripe tomatoes
50 ml extra virgin olive oil
3 cloves garlic, chopped
1 large onion, finely chopped
1 carrot, finely chopped
1 stick celery, finely chopped
100 g leek, finely chopped
A splash of red wine
1 tsp dry oregano
1 handful fresh basil
Water, if required
Salt to taste

1 Blanch the tomatoes in hot water for 5 minutes. Let the tomatoes cool and remove the skin (this is the easiest way to skin a tomato). Chop roughly, taking care to keep the tomato juices.

2 Heat the oil in a pan and cook the garlic and onion together. As soon as the onions become opaque, add the rest of the vegetables, except the tomatoes. Cook for 2 minutes, then add the tomatoes, basil, oregano and the wine. Season with salt and let the mixture simmer on low heat. Add water as and when necessary. I normally cook the sauce for at least an hour on a slow fire, till all the vegetables blend with the sauce.

3 Let the sauce cool, then run it through a blender till it has a thick, creamy consistency.

I add some leek to this sauce although this isn't really kosher. This is because our tomatoes tend to be quite sour at times, and leek mellows the acidity without taking away from the flavour. This sauce too can be frozen for up to 4 weeks easily.

Polenta

In the northern parts of Italy, places like Piedmont, Lombardy and Alto Adige, polenta or cornmeal is a staple. What rice is to Veneto, polenta is to these parts. Slow cooking is the key to good polenta—and it is traditionally cooked in huge copper pans—so make sure you have plenty of time on hand. Cooking style can totally change the way polenta appears. You can have polenta wet (the consistency of mashed potatoes, or porridge) cooked with butter and Parmesan, or have it dry, grilled with a topping of your choice, where it has the solid, crumbly texture of cake. Polenta can even make a wonderful dessert.

200 g polenta flour
1 lt water
500 ml milk
100 g butter
150 g Parmesan grated
Salt to season

1 In a large saucepan, boil the water and milk together. Once it comes to a boil, lower the heat, and slowly start adding the polenta flour in a steady stream, whisking constantly.

2 It will now start bubbling like crazy. Lower the heat and cook on the lowest possible heat for about 25 minutes, till the polenta becomes dense and thick.

3 Add the butter and Parmesan. Serve as a first course or as a side dish.

Sadly it is not so easy to find polenta flour, as yet, but I hope that will change. In cities like Delhi and Mumbai it is available at select stores, but it is worth bringing back some polenta flour if you go abroad on a trip. I love polenta as much as I love my pasta, especially in the winter, when I always end up ordering it either as a side dish or as a first course.

Gnocchi

These little potato dumplings are eaten all over Italy as part of the pasta course. Making gnocchi is not for the faint of heart, but is well worth the effort. And they can be fun to make too, especially if you enlist a friend or two. Every region has its own variations. In Rome they eat gnocchi made of semolina. Gnocchi can be eaten with most pasta sauces, or just by itself, tossed in butter and herbs.

1 kg potatoes
1 egg
300 g flour
50 g Parmesan, grated
Salt & pepper to season

1 Preheat oven to 200°C.

2 Wrap each potato individually in aluminium foil and bake in the oven till tender, say about 40 minutes.

3 Pass the potatoes through a potato ricer or just simply grate them. Don't mash with a fork, as you want the potatoes to have an even texture, without lumps. Add 2 generous pinches of salt and a pinch of pepper to the potatoes. Break the egg and quickly stir it in before it cooks in the warmth of the baked potatoes. Add 2 handfuls of the flour and the Parmesan and mix into the potatoes until absorbed.

4 Turn the potato mixture onto a clean surface and tip the rest of the flour on top. Using your hands, mix the flour into the potatoes. After a minute or two, it will form into dough. Knead the dough lightly. When it reaches a pliable consistency, the dough is ready.

cont. on next page >

5 Sprinkle the surface of the dough with a little flour. Slice small pieces off from the dough ball and roll out into lengths about 1 inch thick. With a knife cut each length of dough into ¾ inch pieces.

6 Place the gnocchi on a tray dusted with a little flour, leaving space between each piece to prevent them from sticking together.

7 Throw the gnocchi into abundant boiling salted water. When the gnocchi rise to the surface, they're ready to serve. Scoop them out with a sieve, shake off the water and transfer them to a tray. Drizzle a little oil over them and give the tray a good shake, so that they are evenly coated and don't stick to each other.

I use baked potato—and always prefer to, even if it means some extra work—because it makes the potato drier and you don't need to use as much flour. However, you can also boil the potatoes, which is quicker than baking them. With boiled potatoes, you will have to use more flour. Again, I add Parmesan to the dough, as it adds that little extra flavour, but you can omit this if you do not have it handy.

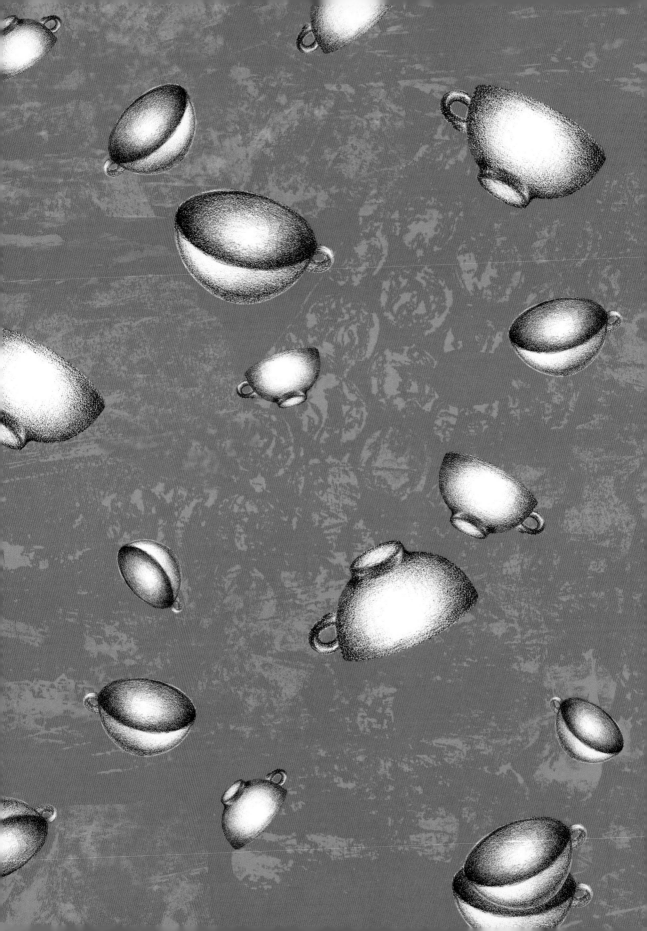

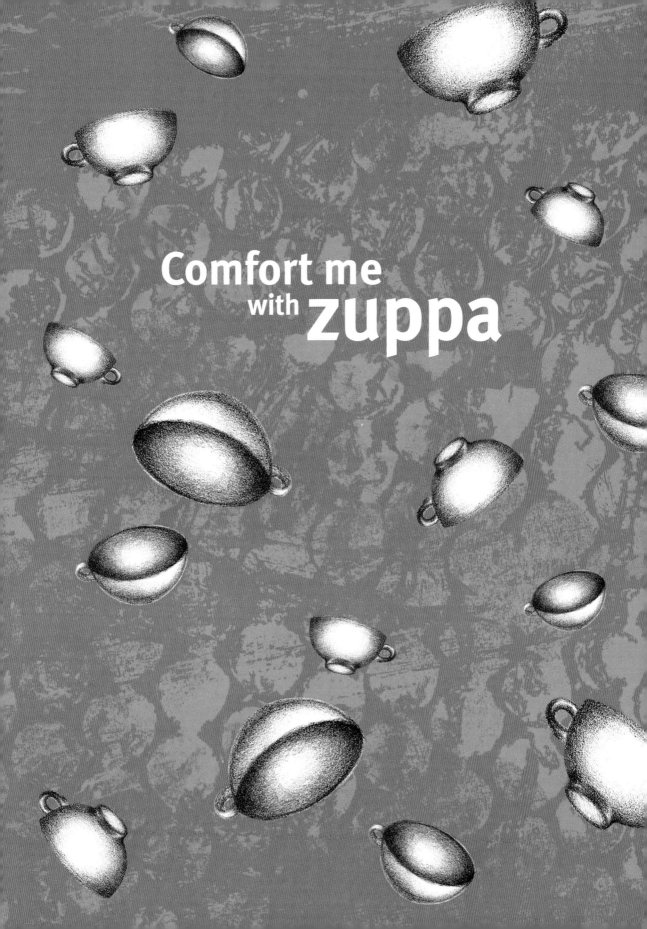

Comfort me
with zuppa

Comfort me
with zuppa

It always amuses me when people tell me how lucky I am to be able to eat such wonderful, fancy food every night. The truth is I am a comfort food girl. My friends always threaten that they will one day leak to the world that I would rather eat daal-chawal than foie gras. Before they do, I confess—yes, it's true. When I do eat at Diva, I normally have a simple spaghetti pomodoro (tomato sauce), or an aglio olio (pasta with garlic and chilli-flavoured oil), or even just a hearty wholesome minestra (soup). Even if I cook for myself, at the end of a very long day I don't have the energy or the inclination to spend a lot of time in the kitchen—which holds true for most of us.

An old adage in Italy says 'La zuppa fa sette cose', or 'soup does seven things'. It is said to quench your thirst, satisfy your hunger, fill your stomach, aid your digestion, make your teeth sparkle, colour your cheeks, and help you sleep. I am not too sure about the sparkling teeth, but soup does have a feel good factor. The perfume of sweet basil in minestrone which has been slow cooking over the fire, will make you feel all warm and fuzzy inside, and that's what you need when you are cooking comfort food—a bowl of something steaming and fragrant, something simple and wholesome tasting, all put together with minimum effort.

All the recipes in this chapter are like a pair of well-worn jeans for me. These are the Italian equivalent of daal-chawal, maach-bhaat, kadhi-chawal and chapati-sabzi; most of these are the core classic home dishes. Easy to cook, heartwarming to taste, they are the perfect way to ease yourself into Italian cooking. In spite of making them so often, I never get bored of them.

A lot of these dishes were on the menu of MezzaLuna, my first restaurant which I opened in 1993 at the age of twenty one. A week before the restaurant was to open, my dear friend Serra came from Italy to check the food for me. She was horrified and described my food as tasting like it had 'come out of cans from American supermarkets'.

The next few days were spent tweaking the menu, making it 'user friendly', as I was told in not-so-kind words by Serra. If I really wanted to pull this off, she said, the food had to be simple, food which could be prepared with what was available in Indian markets at the time, and with, ahem, my limited skills. So this chapter really is my favourite part of the book, for this is where it all began.

Despite their simplicity, all of these recipes reflect the imagination and ingenuity that runs through Italian cooking. Every recipe is usually made from scratch with fresh ingredients, or leftover meats and vegetables from a previous meal. A soup or pasta can be as simple as a vegetable or two cooked with rice or pasta, maybe a fragrant meat broth, or just a simple, grilled fish with a dash of oil and lemon. There is something here for every mood and season. Pasta in broth for a nippy winter night, fish with black pepper for a summer Sunday afternoon with a big salad on the side, chocolate salame—every child's comfort dessert, and risi e bisi; a kind of Italian khichdi.

This is cooking you would want to do on work nights, when you really don't want to slave too much over the stove, nor wonder what's in the fridge. Nor are you cooking for guests, so the pasta pan can go straight onto the table. Many of these recipes are also very friendly on the pocket and don't require many fancy ingredients. Most of what you will need will be in the larder. This chapter is also not about showing off or experimenting. Once you've mastered them, these are dishes that will become staples. Yes, you could easily order a pizza, but why not try pottering around the stove without any pressure? You just might find yourself relaxing while churning out something much nicer than takeaway.

Bruschetta con pomodoro e basilico
Bruschetta with tomato & basil

As the wise say, never scoff at the tried and tested. These Italian 'tamaatar-toasts' will never go out of fashion even though all the top chefs in the world create the most amazing toppings for bruschetta. At our little café at the Italian Cultural Centre, most of the Italians always order these for starters or get a big plate for the table while they wait for their meal. The only thing to ensure here is that the tomatoes are fresh and firm. That's all there is to this great starter—good bread, good olive oil and good tomatoes. This is my take on the traditional recipe.

1 stick baguette (French
  bread), or Italian ciabatta,
  or sliced bread
500 g tomatoes, deseeded
  and chopped
Plenty of basil, shredded
100 ml extra virgin olive oil
4 tbsp black olives,
  finely chopped (optional)
3 cloves garlic, pressed
  slightly with your palm
Salt & pepper to season

1 Heat half the olive oil in a small saucepan and add the garlic cloves. Sauté till golden and set aside. You want the oil to obtain just the perfume of the garlic, without making it too garlicky. Some of my guests ask me to add chopped garlic to their bruschetta, which you could do too if you wish, but it's not very authentic, and more importantly it takes away from the fresh flavour of the tomato.

2 Mix the tomatoes, remaining olive oil, basil and olives in a mixing bowl. Season with salt and pepper.

3 Slice the ciabatta or the baguette into bite-sized slices. Grill the slices in a pan on top of the stove, or under a grill. These also toast fantastically over a barbecue.

4 Brush both sides of the grilled bread with garlic-perfumed oil and top it with the tomato mixture. Drizzle a bit more garlic oil over the tomatoes and serve the bruschetta garnished with whole basil leaves.

> If making bruschetta when entertaining, slice the bread into bite-sized pieces for a cocktail party or half-toast sizes for a sit-down dinner. You can get French baguettes at any half decent bakery. Some of the better bakeries stock ciabatta too.

Minestrone di verdure
Hearty vegetable soup

I think this is the greatest soup ever created. It can work as a great first course for dinner, or as a hearty lunch with a chunk of crusty bread. In Italy minestrone is not only a peasant's meal, but also an aristocrat's comfort food. You can do many variations of it, depending on what you have handy. This is my version, which both my partner Gita and I like very much.

30 ml olive oil
1 medium onion, chopped
100 g carrot, chopped
100 g zucchini, chopped
250 g tomatoes, skinned
  and chopped
1 stick celery, chopped
1 lt vegetable stock or water
1 handful parsley, chopped
Plenty of basil
Plenty of celery leaves, torn
½ kg dried kidney beans,
  cooked
50 g vermicelli or short
  pasta, broken
Grated Parmesan, for topping
Salt & pepper to season

1 Heat the olive oil in a big saucepan, deep enough to hold all the ingredients. Sauté the onion and celery until soft. Add the tomatoes and cook for 5 more minutes. Add the stock or water, and bring to a boil. Throw in all the remaining ingredients except the Parmesan and pasta.

2 Cook on low heat. When the aromas hit your nostrils, in about 20 minutes, add the pasta and cook for another 10 minutes. Season with salt and pepper.

3 Serve hot, drizzled with extra virgin olive oil and grated Parmesan.

This soup tastes even better the following day. I like to cook it in big quantities, as it stays good for a few days and can be frozen for weeks. I have been told by my Italian friends that adding the rind of Parmesan to the stock gives the soup a very nutty and intense flavour, advice I follow at Diva all the time.

Minestrone di zucca

Pumpkin soup | Verona

Though eggplant is my favourite vegetable, I must say pumpkin is a close second. We are lucky, for in India we get pumpkin all through the year. This majestic, golden vegetable is so versatile. I use it as a filling for crepes, for ravioli, and sauces. A classic way to cook pumpkin is to make a soup with it—it looks beautiful and really warms you up. A dear friend likes to add a bit of ginger to it, and swears that it enhances the taste tremendously.

500 g pumpkin, peeled
 and cubed
1 large onion, chopped
1 clove garlic, minced
1 lt chicken stock or water
75 g butter
300 ml milk
1 pinch grated nutmeg
Grated Parmesan (optional)
Salt & pepper to season

1 Season the pumpkin cubes with salt, drizzle with olive oil, place in a baking tray and roast in a preheated oven at 200°C for about 25 minutes.

2 In a large saucepan, melt the butter and cook the onion till pink. Add the garlic, and cook for another minute. Add the roasted pumpkin and water or stock, and let it cook for another 10 minutes. Remove from heat and let the mixture cool down a little.

3 In a blender, purée the soup till it reaches a very fine consistency.

4 Pour into a pan with the milk and heat again. Season with salt, pepper and nutmeg.

5 Serve with grated Parmesan.

Normally raw pumpkin is cooked with onion, but I prefer to roast it in the oven first as this gives the pumpkin a slight smoky flavour. However, if you are short on time, cook the pumpkin directly with the onion. But do remember to cook it a bit longer, till the pumpkin is soft.

Insalata caprese

Classic mozzarella tomato salad | Capri

Fabulous enough for you to show off, simple enough to churn out on a working night, and light enough to eat with your beloved. Representing the three colours of the Italian flag, this salad comes from the island of Capri, in the south of Italy. The ingredients are the same as those used to make the classic Margherita pizza, except here they are in an uncooked, salad form. They say this dish was invented in a trattoria in Capri called Da Vicenzo, and was served for people who were in a hurry during lunchtime.

1 kg firm tomatoes
½ kg fresh mozzarella
Plenty of fresh basil
4 tbsp extra virgin olive oil
Salt & pepper to season

1 Slice the tomato around ¼ inch thick.

2 Slice the mozzarella to the same thickness as the tomato.

3 On a large platter, arrange the red tomato, white mozzarella slices and green basil leaves, alternating and overlapping them, so that you can see all three colours. Drizzle with olive oil and sprinkle with salt and pepper.

4 This salad is flavoured only with olive oil and salt. Don't add vinegar by mistake, for the sharpness of the vinegar will kill its delicate flavours.

> In the bigger metros like Delhi and Mumbai you can also get small-sized mozzarella called bocconcini. If you want to serve this as a snack, impale cherry tomatoes and bocconcini on a toothpick with a basil leaf in the centre. It looks stunning and can be made very quickly.

Pasta con pesto

Pasta with pesto sauce | Originally from Liguria

This simple yet very satisfying pasta can be made within a matter of minutes, provided you have some pesto handy.

1 quantity pesto (p 26)
1 packet long pasta such as
  spaghetti, linguine, bucatini
  or tagliolini
Salt & pepper to season

1 Bring a large pot of salted water to a boil, add the pasta and cook till al dente. Drain in a colander, reserving some pasta water.

2 Place the pesto sauce in a shallow serving bowl. Transfer the pasta to the serving bowl along with some of the cooking water. Toss and serve.

> Rich, intensely flavoured pesto is always diluted with a little of the pasta cooking water when served. Feel free to add tender beans or artichokes, or even potatoes if you want to temper the overpowering taste of basil. The classic Ligurian way to eat this is with beans and small potatoes. The Ligurians use a small corkscrew-shaped pasta called trofie, which is closest to fusilli in shape, with their pesto.

Pasta carbonara

Pasta with a creamy bacon sauce | Rome

This simple Roman pasta dish derives its name from 'carbone', meaning coal. As the story goes, it was a pasta popular with coal miners. The original recipe calls for guanciale, which is pig's cheeks, but since this is not easily available, I use bacon instead.

1 packet spaghetti
100 g bacon, cut in strips
3 eggs
1 egg yolk
100 g Pecorino Romano
  or Parmesan, grated
1 tbsp olive oil
Lots of black pepper,
  coarsely crushed
Salt to taste

1 In a large pan or a saucepan, heat the olive oil and fry the bacon till crisp. Set aside.

2 In a mixing bowl, beat the whole eggs and the yolk well. Stir in the grated cheese and set aside.

3 Boil the spaghetti in abundant salted water. Drain the pasta, reserving some of the cooking water.

4 In another saucepan, toss the pasta with the egg mixture, bacon and any fat rendered from cooking the bacon, over very low heat. Make sure that the individual strands of pasta are all coated properly with the mixture. Season with salt, add the pasta water, give it a quick toss, and remove right away from the heat. The sauce should have a creamy texture, which will be lost if the pasta remains on the fire too long. The idea is to cook the egg with the heat of the pasta, and not with the heat of the fire.

5 Serve right away with lots of pepper, freshly crushed in a pepper mill, and more Parmesan if desired.

> Many of us believe that carbonara is a cream sauce. It is not! The creaminess in the sauce comes from eggs and cheese. If you add cream, you will have a different pasta altogether. A good one, I'm sure, but definitely not a carbonara.

Pasta con pomodoro e basilico
Pasta with basic tomato & basil sauce

This is the most basic pasta sauce and the benchmark of a good Italian cook. It should be cooked fast, on high heat, so that the tomatoes lose their watery quality yet retain their sweetness. Once you have a basic tomato sauce, you can create zillions of variations. Add grilled veggies, slivers of ham, or even some fish or prawns. Just don't add chicken!

1 kg large, red, ripe tomatoes
40 ml extra virgin olive oil
3 cloves garlic, peeled
  and minced
1 handful fresh basil
1 pinch red chilli flakes
1 packet penne
Parmesan
Salt to taste

1 Cut the tomatoes in half, crosswise, and remove most of the seeds, using your fingers. Then quarter the tomatoes.

2 Heat the oil in a large pan, and add garlic and chilli flakes. As soon as the garlic gives off its aroma and becomes opaque, add the tomatoes. Cook over high heat until the tomato begins to thicken. Use a wooden spoon to stir and help break the tomato pulp.

3 Add the basil, either whole or roughly chopped, and salt. When the sauce is cooked, say about another 10 minutes, remove it from the heat and run it through a food processor for about 30 seconds.

4 Cook the pasta in abundant boiling water, till al dente, and drain. Place in a serving bowl with the sauce. Drizzle a little olive oil over the pasta and mix well with the sauce.

5 Serve with grated Parmesan.

> You could use any pasta here—long, thin, short or tube—as this sauce works well with all types of pasta.

Tagliatelle al sugo di agnello
Tagliatelle with meat sauce | Bologna

The classic Bolognese sauce is made with beef, but I have substituted mutton here. You can make this recipe with duck or any red meat. It works well with tagliatelle or penne pasta, and also as a filling for lasagna.

1 packet tagliatelle
30 g butter
70 ml olive oil
25 g bacon, finely chopped
1 onion, finely chopped
2 cloves garlic, minced
100 g carrot, peeled and
  finely chopped
1 stick celery, finely chopped
400 g minced mutton (ask
  the butcher to give you
  mince from leaner meat)
150 ml good red wine, such
  as Grover's La Reserva
  or Sula's Dindori
100 ml milk
400 g canned tomato,
  chopped with the juices
1 bay leaf
1 handful basil, torn
  or thyme
Salt & pepper to taste

1 In a heavy saucepan or a non-stick pan, melt the butter and add the oil over a medium heat. Add the onion and cook for 3 – 4 minutes.

2 Stir in the celery, garlic and carrot, and cook for another couple of minutes. Stir in the meat, making sure it mixes in well with the veggies. Season with salt and pepper.

3 Pour in the wine, increase the flame to high and cook till all the liquid evaporates.

4 Add milk and cook again till all the liquid evaporates. Stir in the tomatoes along with their juice, basil or thyme, reduce the heat to low and let the mixture simmer for about an hour, stirring occasionally. When a heavenly aroma arises, you know the meat sauce is ready.

Penne alla Loredana

Loredana's penne or fusilli with cauliflower | Naples

1 cauliflower
500 g penne or fusilli
100 g bacon, roughly diced
3 tbsp olive oil
2 cloves garlic, whole
1 small red chilli
Parmesan

1 Cut a medium-sized cauliflower into small florets. Place the florets in a pot with 3 litres of cold water and cook very well until the cauliflower is so soft that you can mash it with a spoon, softer than your regular boiled or steamed cauliflower.

2 In a small pan, heat 3 tablespoons of olive oil and add a small red chilli and 2 cloves of garlic. Fry on a slow fire until the garlic is golden, then discard the garlic. Add the bacon to the pan and fry for about 2 minutes.

3 Cook the pasta in boiling, salted water. Strain, leaving a bit of water in the pasta. Add the cooked pasta with its water to the cauliflower, and cook together for a minute.

4 Add the fried bacon with its oil, and grated Parmesan. Mix well, and leave to rest for 3 – 4 minutes, so that the pasta can absorb the flavours of the cheese, bacon and sauce. Buon appetito!

Risi e bisi

Rice & peas | Venice

Risi e bisi means 'rice and peas' in the dialect of Venice. Every child who has grown up in Venice has memories of this classic dish. Giannina, my wonderful Venetian friend (I hope you noticed that I wrote Venetian, and not Italian), always has a sparkle and warmth in her eyes when she speaks of risi e bisi. It is light, colourful, and widely loved.

500 g Arborio rice
1 tbsp olive oil
50 g butter
1 medium onion,
  finely chopped
50 g cooked ham
1 handful parsley
1½ kg fresh peas
1 lt meat stock (p 23)
Parmesan to garnish
Salt & pepper to season

1 Heat the oil and half of the butter together in a pan. Sauté the onion till pink, add ham and parsley.

2 Add the peas and cook for about a minute. Add a ladleful of stock and let it simmer until the peas are almost cooked, for about 10 minutes.

3 Add the rice, cover with stock and cook for 20 – 25 minutes. Season with salt and pepper and serve hot with a generous sprinkling of Parmesan.

As you will notice, this is not the classic risotto, for you are not adding the stock ladle by ladle but cooking this dish just like we would cook our rice. This is a great dish for people who do not want to watch the pot constantly, as one has to when preparing risotto. Vegetarians can remove the ham and use vegetable stock instead; Italian style matar khichdi. If you don't have meat stock cubes handy and don't have the time to prepare fresh stock, you could use vegetable or chicken stock as well.

Torta di riso e spinaci

Spinach & rice tart | Genoa

This simple dish from Liguria is close to my heart. I used to go to Genoa quite often when I was still in the marble business, and there was a little restaurant my client would take me to which had this dish on the menu as an antipasti. I loved it so much that I would order it for my starter and again for my main course.

400 g spinach, stalks
  removed
100 g Arborio rice
1 medium onion, chopped
20 ml olive oil
20 g butter
4 eggs
50 g Parmesan, grated
50 ml single cream
1 pinch grated nutmeg
Vegetable stock for
  cooking risotto (p 24)
Salt & pepper to season

1 Wash the spinach leaves well and blanch in boiling water for a few minutes. Chop roughly and set aside.

2 Preheat oven to 200°C.

3 Prepare the basic risotto (p 6).

4 Add the spinach and half the Parmesan to the risotto. Add cream, nutmeg and eggs and mix well. Season with salt and pepper.

5 Butter a non-stick baking tin. Dust it with Parmesan cheese and pour in the risotto mixture. Bake for about 20 minutes or till it is golden.

6 Remove from mould, cut into wedges, and serve.

> This tart can be eaten either hot or cold. So when you are cooking for that someone special, and don't want to stay too long in the kitchen, this can be prepared beforehand and served as a starter. I make it with many variations. Instead of spinach I sometimes add sautéed mushroom or add a different cheese. It also works well with some ham added to it, and is a great way of using leftover risotto.

Frittata di cipolle e gorgonzola

Italian style cheese & onion omelette | Parma

They say an Italian mama will never let anything go waste—a frittata is a great way of using leftovers from last night's dinner. Frittata, like an omelette, is cooked on the stove in a pan, but finished under a grill. I particularly like the sharp taste of Gorgonzola cheese with the sweetness of onions. However you can make this without the cheese as well, or substitute Gorgonzola with any other cheese you might have handy.

1 tbsp butter
20 ml olive oil
3 medium onions, sliced
8 eggs
75 ml milk
50 g Gorgonzola,
  crumbled (optional)
1 handful thyme or parsley
2 medium potatoes,
  thinly sliced
Pepper to taste

1 In a large pan, heat the butter and olive oil together over medium heat. Add the onions and potatoes to the pan and lower the heat. Cook the onions and potatoes for 10 – 15 minutes or until golden, ensuring that the onions do not turn brown, as that will make them bitter.

2 In a mixing bowl, beat the eggs with the milk and pepper until frothy. Pour the egg mixture over the onions and potatoes, and cover the dish. Now the flame should be medium to low. Cook the frittata about 5 – 6 minutes, until it is almost set.

3 If you are using cheese, spread it over the frittata, cover and cook for another 2 minutes.

4 To finish, place the frittata under the grill for 2 minutes. It will puff up slightly. Allow it to rest for 5 minutes, then cut in wedges and serve.

Frittata can be eaten either hot or at room temperature. Unlike an omelette, it is not folded over and eaten the way it is; rather, it is topped with leftover pasta, onions and cheese, vegetables, ham or sausages. I haven't added any salt here as Gorgonzola is quite a salty cheese. A frittata is normally eaten as part of antipasti or a light lunch. However, there is nothing to stop you from making a hearty frittata for breakfast!

Flan di carote e cavolfiore

Carrot & cauliflower flan | Umbria

This is a delicious vegetarian main course. I ate it as a side dish in a small restaurant in Orvieto, my favourite town in Umbria, and noted it immediately in my little black book. The separation of ingredients and the colour is what lends originality to this dish. I have used two of the vegetables most easily available to us.

500 g carrot
1 head cauliflower
300 g ricotta
75 g Parmesan, grated
75 g butter, melted
1 egg
1 pinch nutmeg
Salt & pepper to season

1 Preheat oven to 200°C.

2 Boil the vegetables separately in abundant salt water. Drain and purée, again separately. The purées should be smooth and creamy. Put the carrot and cauliflower purées in separate bowls.

3 Beat the egg in a small mixing bowl. Add equal amounts of ricotta, Parmesan, melted butter and egg to each purée. Season with salt, pepper and nutmeg.

4 Pour one of the purées into a round cake tin or a buttered flan dish. Let it settle, then slowly pour the second purée on top to achieve two separate layers.

5 Place the tin within a larger baking dish into which you have poured some water. This is called a bain-marie. The water in the larger dish should come halfway up the sides of the tin holding the purées. The idea is that the flan should cook with indirect heat, for about an hour. To check whether it is cooked, insert a toothpick—it should come out clean.

6 Serve with a mixed green salad.

This is really a very simple recipe to follow and is great comfort food. The same recipe can be modified as a starter for a sit-down dinner, if prepared in small, individual tart moulds. Also, you can use broccoli instead of cauliflower.

Pesce alla griglia
Simple grilled fish

I am yet to meet an Italian who does not eat fish. Italians do their fish very well, cooking it simply rather than drowning it with sauces and seasonings. During festive times like Christmas, it is fish and not meat that takes precedence on the table. This recipe comes from a girl I knew called Elena. She used to live in Genoa, working two jobs, yet she always found a few minutes to grill fish and serve it to me with a big salad.

600 g fillet of any firm
 white flesh fish, like red
 snapper, sole or bekti

MARINADE
50 ml extra virgin olive oil
2 tbsp lemon juice
1 clove garlic, minced
A few sprigs of fresh
 rosemary or oregano
1 tbsp pesto (p 26)
Salt & pepper to season

1 Mix all the ingredients for the marinade in a mixing bowl and give it a good whisk. Add the cleaned fish fillet to the marinade, making sure it is well coated. Cover and keep in the fridge for a couple of hours to let the flavours soak into the fish. In case you are tired and hungry and want a quick bite, you can safely leave this step out.

2 Grill the fish on medium flame in a non-stick pan, basting regularly with the marinade. Allow 2 – 3 minutes for each side, depending on the thickness of the fillet. Eat right away with a squeeze of lemon and a big salad.

On nights when I don't have pesto handy, I skip the pesto and it still tastes great. If you have the time you can always make pesto and store it, but now the readymade ones in the market are not too bad either, especially as in this case you are using pesto as a part of the flavouring and not as the main sauce itself.

Pollo alla valdostana

Chicken breast with Parma ham & Fontina | Valley of Aosta

This simple chicken dish, originally from the Valle d'Aosta in the north of Italy, used to feature in my MezzaLuna menu and was loved by everyone. It has all the ingredients we Indians love—cheese, ham and chicken!

500 g chicken breasts, without skin
100 g Parma ham, thinly sliced
1 tbsp flour
1 handful parsley, finely chopped
30 ml olive oil
30 g butter
100 g Fontina cheese, sliced or grated
50 ml dry white wine, like a Sauvignon Blanc
Salt & pepper to season

1 Place the chicken breasts between two sheets of grease-proof paper and beat them flat with a rolling pin. Coat the flattened chicken pieces in flour, parsley, salt and pepper.

2 Heat the butter and olive oil in a shallow pan and cook the chicken on both sides for about 3 – 5 minutes.

3 Place a slice of ham on top of each piece of grilled chicken, and top the ham with sliced or grated Fontina cheese.

4 Pour wine into the pan, cover and simmer for 5 minutes. Serve right away.

> The original recipe calls for Fontina cheese, which is available at select stores, but you could also use Gruyère. There is no substitute for Parma ham, in my opinion, however, if you use cooked ham slices this will still taste great, except it will not be pollo alla valdostana.

Pollo con funghi e pepe nero

Chicken with black pepper & mushroom | Venice

This recipe is very useful when Gita and I go on a weight-loss plan and I have to think of lean meat dishes which still taste fabulous. That's the time when all my Italian chicken recipes come in handy at home.

8 chicken breasts,
  without skin
1 clove garlic, minced
30 ml olive oil
500 g mixed mushrooms
1 handful parsley, chopped
1 medium onion, finely
  chopped
100 ml chicken or
  vegetable stock
75 ml red wine
Salt & pepper to season

1 In a non-stick pan, heat the oil on a very high flame. Brown the chicken breasts on both sides, and set aside.

2 In the same pan, sauté the onion and garlic, add the mushrooms, and cook on a high flame for 5 minutes. Add the wine, stock, salt, pepper and parsley, and bring to a boil. Add the browned chicken, cover and cook over slow heat till the sauce reduces and the chicken cooks through, about 20 minutes.

3 To serve, place a chicken breast on a plate and spoon the mushroom sauce on top. Eat it with loads of sautéed spinach. This is a very healthy and delicious meal.

I always keep some dry porcini mushrooms with me, so instead of stock, I add water in which porcini mushrooms have been soaked. I recommend you do the same if you can get hold of porcini.

Macedonia di frutta
Italian fruit salad

Italians are not very big on desserts and normally they end a meal with fruit. All restaurants have an option of fruit for dessert. This is understandable, for after a starter, a pasta, fish or meat, it is a bit difficult to tuck into yet another course.

1 kg fresh seasonal fruit,
  such as apricots, peaches,
  plums, strawberries, bananas,
  kiwi, melon, mangoes
4 tbsp honey (optional)
1 bottle good light white wine,
  like Chenin Blanc
100 g sugar

1 Cut the pieces of fruit into bite-sized pieces. Place in a large bowl and add the sugar. The sugar draws the juices out of the fruit and sweetens the wine, so don't worry about calories here and be generous with it. Stir the sugar into the fruit gently, without breaking it. Cover with white wine, stir again and let it sit for a couple of hours.

2 Serve the fruit salad chilled, drizzled with honey. If you are in the mood to splurge, serve it with mascarpone or a scoop of vanilla ice cream.

> The wine blends with the juices of the fruit to create a fabulous wine cooler! So if you want to create a nice, light drink, pour in some extra wine.

Salame dolce

Chocolate salame | Originally from Piedmont

This is supposed to be every child's favourite desert in Italy, but I have seen many adults gobble up this amazing desert with the same gusto. And another thing—this is one kind of salami which even my vegetarian Marwari clan likes to eat!

150 g Marie biscuits,
  roughly crumbed,
  or Italian amaretti
50 g sugar
120 g melted butter
2 egg yolks
6 tbsp unsweetened
  cocoa powder
A splash of Amaretto or
  Grand Marnier (optional)

1 Melt the butter and let it cool.

2 Beat the egg yolks with the sugar until the mixture resembles cake batter. Add the melted butter and cocoa powder to make a smooth consistency, like a rich, thick chocolate sauce.

3 Crush the Marie biscuits in a food processor, or with a rolling pin, leaving some pieces a little larger than others so they resemble the speckles of fat in salami.

4 Mix the crushed biscuits into the chocolate mixture. Shape the mix into a salami-like log, and roll it in aluminium foil. Place in the freezer for 30 minutes, or until firm. Unwrap and slice. Serve with soft whipped cream or ice cream, or just eat it by itself.

> Sometimes I add melted dark chocolate instead of cocoa powder. It does make the salami heavier, but for people who love chocolate, it is even yummier. If you want to do that, substitute cocoa powder with 100 g of melted chocolate. You can also add chopped nuts if you want a fancier version.

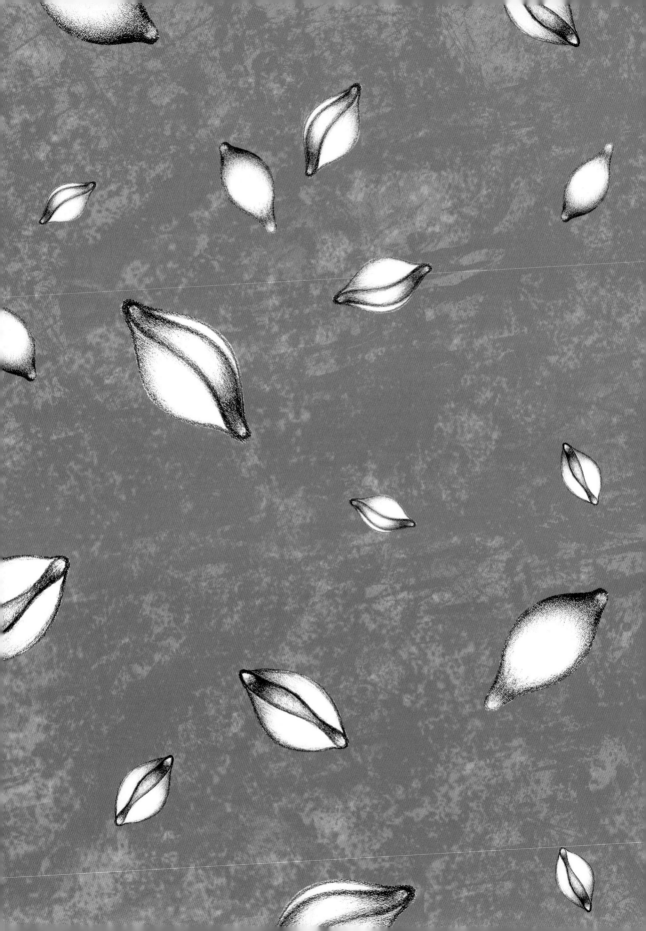

Cooking with
friends

Cooking with
friends

I don't think I would have ever taken up cooking as a profession if I had listened to my childhood friends.

They had always laughed at my unlikely passion for cooking. One day, when I was in Class Ten, I decided to cook them a feast and silence them all. I had been given a simple handbook on Italian cooking and after carefully going through it, decided to invite three of my closest buddies home for an Italian meal. I had gone through a great deal of effort to source the ingredients. In the '80s, even packaged spaghetti was a rare commodity in India. Luckily my father was travelling abroad at the time, and I had given him an ambitious list (our usual food requests to him used to be Kraft cheese and fondue packets!)

The meal was a disaster. After their first bite, my friends were hysterical with laughter. My al dente risotto was proclaimed 'raw khichdi', the spaghetti was strange noodles without any vegetables or sauce. And the salad? Unbelievable! No mayonnaise in the dressing? The only thing they did not mind was the tiramisu, and that was because they hoped to get drunk on it. Fortunately I have always been able to laugh at myself, and so did not mind the weeks of teasing that followed. My friends still moan about how much they suffered as my guinea pigs, and I always respond by saying that they never had much of a palate.

We all might joke about it, but even now having friends over for a meal remains a joy. When you are cooking for friends, the attitude is relaxed. No one is in a hurry, the gossip and laughter goes on and on, while everyone lingers on their starters. You saunter into the kitchen whenever you are ready to prepare the main course while your friends ensure that your wine glass is never empty.

Cooking together with your friends can be as much as fun as cooking for them. You might be pan-frying the fish, trying to be heard above the sizzle and hiss; your buddy is in the meantime chopping the onion, slowly. Someone will be whisking the oil and the vinegar together for the salad and all those who don't like to cook are in the meantime laying the table, lighting the candles and making sure the right music is playing. A word of caution here—you have to be very careful who you are cooking with. I would never dare to cook with Serra, who won't let me stir the risotto even a second too long. When she cooks, her friends are just supposed to enjoy what she makes, and not potter around the kitchen.

Here is an eclectic mix of recipes which my friends and I always cook for each other. You can rustle up most of these effortlessly but they are also one step up from the basic recipes we began with. The ingredients are more special, the dishes a little more unusual, yet the emphasis is still on low effort. Some of the recipes need advance preparation and then can be quickly put together just as you serve your meal. Some, like the lasagna recipes, simply need to be put in the oven so you don't have to fuss in the kitchen while your friends have arrived.

Gamberetti marinati

Anna's marinated prawns | Sicily

This is a great way to start a long and happy meal with friends. Prepare these ahead of time, and polish them off together while you and your friends cook the main course.

450 g prawns, cleaned,
  deveined and lightly
  boiled for 2 – 3 minutes till
  just undercooked
½ cup fresh lemon juice
½ cup fresh orange juice
1 small clove garlic, minced
¼ cup olive oil
3 tbsp limoncello, or lemon-
  flavoured Smirnoff (optional)
1 handful parsley, chopped
Salt & pepper to season

1 Place the prawns in a glass dish. Combine the lemon and orange juices and pour over the prawns. Marinate the prawns in the juices and let them stand for at least 30 minutes, turning the prawns a couple of times.

2 Drain the prawns and discard the marinade. Toss the prawns with garlic, olive oil and salt to taste. Sprinkle with parsley and eat right away.

Mozzarella carrozza

Mozzarella in a carriage | Campania

There is an Italian restaurant called La Famiglia, a few doors away from Vama, my Indian restaurant in London. I couldn't afford to eat at La Famiglia in the early days of Vama but I could never resist treating myself to these fried mozzarella bites. Now I like to make these delicious appetizers from Campania at home, especially when I want to indulge myself and don't have too many fancy ingredients at hand.

8 slices white bread,
  crust removed
500 g mozzarella,
  thinly sliced
50 g flour
4 eggs
Salt & pepper to season
Oil for frying (pomace
  or a good vegetable oil)

1 Place 4 slices of bread on the counter. Top with the mozzarella slices, trimming the cheese to ensure that it does not extend over the edges of the bread. Cover with the 4 remaining slices of bread, making 4 sandwiches in all.

2 Spread the flour on a plate. Pour a cup of water into a shallow bowl.

3 First dip the 4 edges of each sandwich in the flour, then dip the edges in the water, being careful to moisten only the edges and not the inside of the sandwiches. The idea is to form a sort of glue with flour and water that will prevent the mozzarella from leaking out once it melts in the hot oil, as the sandwiches are frying. Arrange the 4 sealed sandwiches on a platter in a single layer.

4 In a small bowl, beat the eggs with the salt and pepper. Pour half of the egg mixture over the sandwiches and set aside for 10 minutes. Turn the sandwiches over and repeat the process on the other side of the sandwiches. The purpose is to allow the bread to soak in the egg as much as possible.

5 Heat the oil in a deep pan. This should be enough for the mozzarella sandwiches to totally sink into the oil. Deep-fry 1 or 2 sandwiches at a time until golden on both sides, turning once, about 3 minutes per batch. Remove with a slotted spoon onto a platter lined with paper towels and blot dry. Cut each sandwich in half and serve hot, with basic tomato sauce (p 27) or with a bowl of pesto (p 26) for dipping.

Panzanella

Bread salad | Tuscany

This delicious Tuscan bread salad, ideal for summer, does not follow a particular recipe. The two ingredients which do not change are tomatoes and bread, the rest depends on my mood and kitchen inventory. Every time I make it, the recipe evolves. At the moment I like this version best, but who knows what will happen the next time I make this wonderful summer salad? An ideal dish to prepare ahead of time—get your friends to add the finishing touches!

1 kg large, fresh, juicy
  tomatoes
1 medium cucumber
100 g small, mild olives
1 medium onion, sliced
100 g sun-dried tomatoes
  and their oil
1 handful oregano, chopped
A few basil leaves, chopped
1 handful parsley, chopped
2 cloves garlic, finely chopped
5 tbsp olive oil
2 tbsp good balsamic vinegar
1 pinch sugar
Salt & pepper
1 loaf Italian ciabatta or
  French baguette, torn
  into pieces

1 Chop the tomatoes and cucumber roughly into 1 cm cubes, and place in a large bowl. Stir in all the remaining ingredients except the bread, and taste for seasoning. Add some lemon juice if you want a more tart salad. Put the salad in the fridge and leave, covered, overnight until you are ready to eat. The flavours will meld into something magical.

2 Immediately before serving, tear the bread into small pieces and stir it into the salad. This salad is great with a chilled glass of Prosecco and lots of sunshine.

> Sometimes I toast the bread slightly and also add some red and yellow peppers. The key to this salad is that the tomatoes have to be juicy. If they aren't, just add a few spoons of tomato juice to the salad.

Insalata Cesare alla Ela

Caesar's salad Ela's way | Rome

My friend Ela is an expert on Caesar's salad. She has to order this great salad whenever she sees it on a menu, and I don't think there are many places that have met with her approval. Thanks to her, I was forced to grow romaine leaves, a waxier variety of lettuce with long leaves, used for this salad. Unfortunately, it is impossible to find romaine leaves in India. Use normal lettuce instead, which works quite well—just don't use iceberg lettuce. According to the divine Ms Ela, a glass of Pinot Grigio works best with Caesar's salad; unless you have some Prosecco handy.

FOR THE CROUTONS
2 large garlic cloves
Pinch of salt
3 tbsp virgin olive oil
2 cups French baguette slices
  cut into ½ inch cubes
  (white bread works too)

FOR THE SALAD
1 large egg
1 tsp fresh lemon juice
30 ml white wine vinegar
30 ml red wine
2 garlic cloves, crushed
1 tsp Dijon mustard
1 tsp Tabasco or even
  Chinese chilli paste
1 tsp Worcestershire sauce
50 ml extra virgin olive oil
2 heads romaine or
  regular lettuce
Plenty of Parmesan, grated
Salt & pepper to season

1 Preheat oven to 200°C.

2 Combine garlic, oil, salt and bread cubes in a bowl. Mix until cubes are coated evenly. Spread the coated cubes onto a baking sheet and bake until the croutons are golden, about 10 minutes. Alternately, toss the cubes in a pan on a high flame, till crisp.

3 Mix the Worcestershire sauce, chilli/Tabasco sauce, wine, vinegar, lemon juice, garlic, salt, pepper and mustard in a bowl. Break the egg and add in. Whisk until smooth.

4 Now comes the tricky part. Slowly add the oil in a steady stream, constantly whisking the dressing, until smooth. Add a bit of Parmesan. You are, in essence, making a fancy mayonnaise (which is made whisking oil into a beaten egg) in 5 minutes. As with normal mayonnaise, if you add the oil too quickly, it will remain separate from the dressing. What has always worked is using my fingers instead of an electrical whisk. And another trick is to immerse the egg in hot water for 30 seconds before cracking it open. This changes the taste of the dressing but ensures the egg won't curdle.

5 Tear the lettuce leaves into 1 – 2 inch pieces, and add them to a large bowl (preferably wooden). Add half the dressing, toss the salad, add the remaining dressing, loads of Parmesan and warm croutons and toss again. Serve on chilled plates.

> The trick to this salad is 'extra garlic, no anchovies' but feel free to add minced anchovy to the dressing if you like. Ela also likes to use herbed salt here, which is not available in India, but you could add a handful of chopped, fresh parsley instead.

Penne al funghi porcini
Serra's penne with porcini | Liguria

In the days before foreign produce was available in Indian markets, Serra would come to visit with some fresh and dry porcini, and a bottle of nice, heavy red wine, and cook this wonderful pasta for us. Porcini, with its almost phallic shape, earthy smells and firm texture, is God's gift to Italy. As William Black writes in his book *Al Dente*, 'tasting fresh porcini should be on everyone's must-taste-before-I-die list'. Fresh porcini is not yet available in India, but I use dried porcini all the time. It sometimes works even better than fresh porcini.

1 packet penne
50 g dried porcini
1 small onion, finely chopped
1 stick celery, finely chopped
½ tsp flour
100 ml warm water
½ tsp butter
1 tsp olive oil
1 handful parsley, chopped
Salt & pepper to season

1 Soak the porcini in warm water for at least 2 – 3 hours.

2 Cook the penne till al dente. While the pasta is boiling, prepare the sauce.

3 In a shallow pan, add butter and olive oil and sauté the onion and celery over a medium flame. Add the flour, porcini and the water in which the porcini was soaked. Cook till the sauce is smooth and has the consistency of single cream. Season with salt, pepper and parsley. Add the pasta and serve right away with grated Parmesan or Pecorino.

Sometimes, when I do not have porcini with me, I make this pasta with dried shiitake mushrooms. Its flavour is not as intense as porcini's but shiitake still works very well. Thyme also works very well in this pasta—thyme and mushroom being a classic combination—so if you have access to fresh thyme, use that instead of parsley.

Gnocchi di spinaci e ricotta
Spinach & ricotta gnocchi with butter & basil | Amalfi

This is a lighter version of regular gnocchi, as it doesn't use potatoes. And unlike the other gnocchi, which goes well with most sauces, these spinach gnocchi have to be paired with the right one. They taste best with a simple butter sauce, but could also work with a simple tomato sauce. But please don't serve these with a mushroom sauce!

1 kg spinach
300 g ricotta
50 g flour
1 egg
1 egg yolk
30 g Parmesan, grated
50 g butter
1 handful basil or sage
Salt & nutmeg to season

1 Boil and chop the spinach, squeezing out as much water as you can.

2 Mix flour with spinach, ricotta, eggs, grated Parmesan and grated nutmeg to form a dough. The gnocchi dough has to be soft, but not sticky. Form the gnocchi, as in the basic gnocchi recipe (p 31). They should be very small and dainty.

3 Cook the gnocchi in boiling water. They are ready when they come up to the surface.

4 Melt some butter in a small pan and add the fresh basil or sage leaves. Toss the gnocchi in the butter sauce and serve with grated Parmesan.

Polenta alla griglia con funghi misti
Grilled polenta with mushroom | Milan

For me, polenta is a wonderful canapé base for parties, a great lunch for a winter afternoon, and an even better side dish. In a way you can play around with it the way you would with pasta or risotto or even bread. This recipe is from Trattoria Milanese, a small restaurant in Milan which only serves Milanese specialities. Normally they make a wet polenta with beef, but once in a while you will find grilled polenta with mushroom and Parmesan shavings. My mouth is already watering as I write this.

Basic polenta (p 30)
500 g mushroom, sliced
50 ml olive oil
1 small onion, finely chopped
1 pinch grated nutmeg
50 g Parmesan cheese
1 handful parsley, chopped
A splash of any white wine
Salt & pepper to season

1 Make the polenta according to the basic polenta recipe (p 30), minus the Parmesan.

2 When ready, spread it on a large tray or back of a plate. It should be about half an inch thick. Leave till it is cold and cut into wedges or squares.

3 Brush both sides of the polenta with olive oil, and grill either on a pan or under a very hot grill. Keep aside.

4 In a pan, heat the olive oil and sauté the onion and mushroom till brown. Add the parsley, wine and nutmeg. Let it all cook for another 5 minutes. Season with salt and pepper.

5 In a plate place the polenta square or wedge, and spoon the mushroom mixture on top. Serve with Parmesan shavings which you can make using a vegetable peeler.

> You could top this with slivers of Parma ham, or with some salad leaves or with sautéed spinach and pine nuts. Another variation is to grill the polenta with Gorgonzola or any cheese of your choice. For a party you could make bite-size squares of polenta, with various toppings, and pass them around as an appetiser, with your drinks.

Verdure alla griglia
Roasted grilled vegetables

2 yellow bell peppers,
  quartered
2 red bell peppers,
  quartered
1 zucchini, sliced either
  lengthwise or in rounds
1 eggplant, sliced lengthwise
  or in rounds
2 tbsp olive oil
2 tbsp basil, shredded
Salt to season

1 Preheat the oven to the highest point.

2 Set peppers, zucchini and eggplant on a baking sheet, and brush with a tablespoon of olive oil. Bake for about 20 minutes, until the skin begins to blister. Place the peppers (not the zucchini and eggplant) in a plastic bag, to steam for a few minutes. This helps to separate the skin. Pull the skin off the peppers, remove the stems, and open out to remove the seeds and membranes. Tear the peppers into 4 – 6 pieces each.

3 Lay the peeled peppers, zucchini and eggplant on a flat serving plate. In a small bowl, combine olive oil, basil and salt to taste, and pour over the roasted vegetables. You can add a bit of chopped garlic, to enhance the flavours. Serve with toasted bread brushed with olive oil.

Lasagne con il pesto e patate

Lasagne with pesto & potatoes | Liguria

Lasagne or any baked pasta is great when friends are coming over. These are hearty dishes, and can be prepared beforehand. There are not many people who dislike a good lasagna. This one has an unusual filling of potato and pesto.

1 packet lasagna sheets
100 g pesto (p 26)
100 g béchamel (p 25)
2 medium potatoes, boiled
  and thinly sliced
Salt to season
Extra virgin olive oil
Loads of grated Parmesan

1 Preheat oven to 180°C.

2 In a pan, toss the potato and pesto over medium heat for less than a minute. Set aside.

3 Boil the lasagna sheets in abundant salted water for 4 – 5 minutes. Do not over cook as these will cook further in the oven.

4 Pour some extra virgin olive oil on a small baking tray, and cover the surface with lasagna sheets. Put some pesto potatoes on the lasagna, then pour some béchamel. Continue making layers of lasagna, potato pesto and béchamel, finishing with a layer of béchamel. Sprinkle with grated Parmesan. Bake in the oven for about 20 minutes.

> Try potato and Gorgonzola as an alternate filling and you'll have lasagne bianco, or white lasagne, also very nice but much heavier.

Carbonara alle zucchine

Zucchini carbonara | Rome

Gianna Gastaldi has the best Italian table in Delhi and every Italian in the city knows of her skill. When I opened the café at the Italian Cultural Centre in Delhi, my well-wishers had only one word of caution—'Make sure it meets Madam Gastaldi's approval.' Gianna is known to adapt Italian recipes to whatever is available at INA Market in New Delhi, and this is one of her signature dishes—an elegant, yet simple, variation of the classic carbonara.

400 g penne rigate
400 g zucchini, cut into
 julienne strips
2 onions, finely chopped
4 tbsp extra virgin olive oil
2 eggs
120 g Parmesan
Salt & pepper to season

1 Bring 3 litres of salted water to a boil in a large pot. Boil the pasta and cook until al dente.

2 In a saucepan heat the olive oil, add the chopped onions and cook for 2 minutes. Add the zucchini, season with salt and pepper, and continue to cook for 5 minutes. Don't allow the vegetables to colour. Remove the pan from the heat and set aside.

3 Break the eggs into a jug, add 70 g of Parmesan, salt and pepper, and beat well to mix.

4 Drain the pasta, put it into the sauté pan with the zucchini, add the beaten eggs and a tablespoon of the pasta cooking water, and toss for 2 minutes.

5 Put the pasta in a serving bowl, top with Parmesan, and serve immediately.

Risotto di zucca con pancetta croccante

Pumpkin & crispy bacon risotto | Verona

In Italy they say risotto is perfect when cooked all'onda, which means 'like waves'—perfectly creamy, not too liquid and not too hard. If I may humbly submit here, the last risotto I prepared for a group of friends who came for lunch was sublime—like the waves.

100 g bacon
250 g pumpkin, peeled
  and cubed
1 medium onion, chopped
Basic risotto recipe (p 6)
2 tbsp extra virgin olive oil
A few sprigs of rosemary
50 g Grana Padano or
  Parmesan, grated

1 Chop the bacon into small cubes. Sauté in a pan till crispy, and set aside.

2 Cook the onion and pumpkin, in the bacon fat remaining in the pan, till the pumpkin is tender. Puree the pumpkin in a blender until smooth.

3 Add the puree to the basic risotto after the rice has been coated with wine. Season with salt and pepper. When the rice is cooked, serve with a drizzle of olive oil, rosemary sprigs, crispy bacon and a sprinkle of grated cheese.

Pollo ripieno con mascarpone

Chicken stuffed with mascarpone | Umbria

This is a very simple recipe, and provided you have the ingredients handy, can be prepared very quickly. It can be cooked in a pan, in an oven, and is delicious broiled over charcoal if you have fired the barbecue for your Sunday brunch.

1 kg chicken breast
100 g mascarpone
50 ml olive oil
1 clove garlic, minced
Salt & pepper to season

FOR THE SAUCE
100 ml chicken stock (p 23)
Juice of 1 lime
50 ml white wine
1 pinch red chilli flakes
25 ml olive oil
1 tbsp butter
Salt & pepper to season

1 Mix the oil, salt, pepper and minced garlic together in a mixing bowl. Coat the chicken breasts evenly with this marinade.

2 Slit the chicken breast lengthways to create a pocket. Put a spoon of mascarpone into the pocket, close it and reseal the breast with a toothpick. Repeat with all the chicken breasts. Set aside.

3 To make the sauce, melt the oil and butter together in a pan. Add the wine, chicken stock and lemon juice. Throw in the chilli flakes, season with salt and let the sauce simmer while the chicken is being cooked.

4 Cook the chicken in a preheated 200°C oven for about 10 – 12 minutes, in a pan or on a barbecue. Pour a spoon of sauce over each cooked chicken breast and serve.

Mascarpone works as a tenderiser for the chicken and has a very subtle flavour. Also, if you like, you could add sliced tomatoes with mascarpone to the stuffing.

Pesce con olive e pomodoro

Fresh fish with olive & tomato | Naples

This dish is yet another example of how easy it is to cook fish elegantly in Italian cooking. Mrs Rossi, who used to work at the Italian Embassy in New Delhi, gave me this recipe. She wanted me to prepare it for one of her parties and made sure the recipe was sent beforehand, just in case I did something wrong! This recipe is very light on the stomach, so great for when you are on a diet.

1 kg fresh fish fillet like sole
  or red snapper
1 kg potatoes
2 medium white onions,
  finely sliced
500 g tomatoes, deseeded,
  skinned and chopped
40 ml extra virgin olive oil
Lots of black olives, pitted
1 handful fresh oregano,
  or 1 tbsp dried oregano
Salt & pepper to season

1 Preheat oven to 200°C.

2 Peel and very thinly slice the potatoes. Grease a large baking dish with olive oil, place the sliced potatoes in it, drizzle with more oil, season with salt and bake for about 20 minutes.

3 Remove from the oven, cover with chopped tomatoes and sliced onions and season with salt. Place the fish fillet on top and cover with olives and oregano. Season with salt and pepper. The fish slices should just nestle very comfortably into the potato, tomato and onion mixture. Pour a generous amount of olive oil on top and bake again for about 20 minutes. Serve hot.

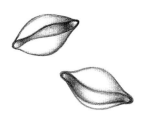

Agneletto brodettato

Lamb with egg & lemon sauce | Rome

This is a typical lamb dish seen on a Roman table during Easter. Italian Jewish cooking uses eggs to thicken the sauce, and this is one of the quintessential dishes in Roman-Jewish cuisine.

1 kg shoulder of mutton,
  cut into cubes (ask the
  butcher to do it)
2 limes
50 ml olive oil
100 ml any white wine
50 g ham, chopped
3 egg yolks
1 onion, chopped
1 handful parsley, chopped
1 pinch dried marjoram
  (which is widely available,
  if not use dried oregano)
Salt & pepper to season

1 Rub the lamb with half a lime. Wash, and dry the meat with kitchen towel.

2 In a large saucepan, heat the olive oil, add the ham and onion, and brown the lamb. Season with salt and pepper.

3 When the lamb is evenly browned, add the white wine. Cook till tender, about an hour over a low heat, adding a few spoonfuls of hot water if the meat is drying out.

4 Beat the egg yolks in a bowl with chopped parsley and marjoram, a tsp of grated lime peel and the juice of a whole lime.

5 When the lamb has finished cooking, turn off the heat and pour the egg mixture over it. Stir and let the eggs coagulate, but do not let them set too hard.

6 Serve with a green salad or baby potatoes.

Saltimbocca

Veal scallops with Parma ham & sage | Rome

Saltimbocca is a Roman specialty and literally means 'jumps in the mouth'. My friend Sabrina, who is from the region, cooked her version of saltimbocca for us when she was visiting last year. That's why I love having friends over from Italy. I always suggest they cook for us one night. That way I learn something new and don't have to slave in the kitchen for one evening! You could easily prepare this with pork fillet, and even chicken breast.

12 small veal scallops,
  the size of your palm
12 slices of raw ham
  (Parma ham crudo)
Sage
60 g butter
Salt to taste
½ cup dry white wine like
  Sauvignon Blanc

1 Place the scallops between two sheets of grease-proof paper and beat them to soften and thin them. Place a slice of ham and one sage leaf on each flattened scallop, and run a toothpick through all three to hold them together.

2 Melt the butter in a pan over a low fire. Add the scallops and brown them on both sides (it takes a few minutes). Add salt with care, as the ham is already salty. If you wish you can add pepper too. Pour the wine over it all. Serve the scallops warm, the ham and sage facing up.

> When I cooked this at home, I placed a thin strip of cheese on top, but this was just an inspiration for that evening. The traditional recipe does not call for cheese. Also, you can replace the butter with oil.

Lasagne con ragu di agnello

Lasagne with meat sauce | Rome

Lasagne is another Italian dish most Indians have heard of—but I am not sure how many have tasted an authentic one. It's an ideal dish to cook for friends as you can cook the sauces beforehand, assemble it at the last moment and forget about it while it bakes.

500 g meat sauce (p 48)
200 ml béchamel (p 25)
400 g lasagna sheets
20 g butter
70 g grated Parmesan

1 Preheat the oven at 180°C.

2 Prepare the béchamel and the meat sauce.

3 Blanch the pasta sheets in abundant salted water for about 5 minutes, no more, since the pasta sheets will also cook in the oven with the sauce.

4 Grease a baking tray with a bit of butter, and arrange a single layer of pasta sheet, top it with meat sauce, then béchamel and grated Parmesan. Repeat till you have three layers. The final topping should be of Parmesan. Dot it with the remaining butter and bake for about 30 – 35 minutes.

> Truth be told, lasagne can be difficult to make. But you can easily make it when you have some leftover meat sauce. There are many variations you could do with the fillings—adding sliced grilled eggplant, or sausages, spinach and ricotta—but this really is the most wholesome, and a classic. Many Italian friends argue that lasagne should be assembled a day in advance, for the flavours to develop, and baked only a day later.

Ciambella alle mele

Apple ring cake | Italian Alps - Trentino

This is one of those classic recipes which is passed from grandmother to granddaughter, from one friend to another. I was given it by my friend Elena. This is truly my comfort dessert. Sometimes I bake it in the middle of the night when I get the urge to eat something sweet. Although making a cake is fairly labour intensive, this is surprisingly simple to make. All you need is a bowl to mix all the ingredients in and a baking tin. The whole thing takes under an hour. It is the perfect cake to bake with friends as you don't really need to be concentrating while you make it.

4 apples
4 eggs
150 g sugar
300 g flour
80 ml olive oil
250 g natural yoghurt
2 tsp baking powder
1 tbsp orange zest
 (orange peel, without
 the bitter white pith)
1 pinch salt
1 pinch cinnamon
 (optional)

1 Preheat oven to 180°C.

2 Peel, quarter and thinly slice the apples.

3 Beat the eggs with the sugar until light and very foamy. Fold in, one at a time, the flour, oil, sliced apples, yoghurt, baking powder, salt and orange zest. Add cinnamon if you want to spice it up a bit. Mix well until smooth.

4 Grease a ring mould (easily available) with olive oil and dust it with a bit of flour. Pour the mixture into the mould and bake for about 40 minutes. Serve warm or at room temperature.

> You can also do a ciambella of banana, substituting the apple with 6 puréed bananas.

Torta di ricotta

Ricotta cake | Sicily

Another really easy, all-in-one cake.

1 kg ricotta
30 g fine bread crumbs
150 g sugar
7 large eggs
1 orange peel, grated
50 g semi-sweet
  chocolate chips
50 g pine nuts
50 g raisins
2 tsp flour

1 Put the ricotta in a mixing bowl, add the sugar and eggs, and process in a food processor or blender till you have a smooth mixture.

2 Add the orange peel, chocolate chips, raisins, pine nuts and flour.

3 Preheat oven to 200°C.

4 Generously butter a baking pan and sprinkle with bread crumbs. Pour the ricotta mixture into the prepared pan, and bake for 1 hour until lightly golden. The centre should feel slightly firm and should begin to crack.

5 Take the cake out of the oven and let the cake cool. Remove from pan and serve dusted with sugar.

Tiramisu
The 'pick-me-up' cake

No Italian cookbook can be complete without a tiramisu recipe. Every Italian I have met has their own version. Here is the recipe which works well for me. Tiramisu should be made with mascarpone, which is available at selected stores. In case you can't find mascarpone, substitute with unsalted Philadelphia cream cheese.

2 egg yolks
2 tbsp caster sugar
250 g mascarpone or
   cream cheese
175 ml strong black coffee
   (175 ml water with
   2 tbsp coffee)
A few drops of vanilla
   essence (optional)
3 tbsp brandy
150 g sponge fingers, or
   sponge cake cut into fingers
Cocoa powder for dusting

1 In a bowl, beat the egg yolks and sugar together till the mixture becomes light and creamy.

2 Add the vanilla essence and fold in the mascarpone.

3 Make strong black coffee and mix the brandy into the coffee. Quickly dip the sponge fingers in the coffee-brandy mix, just enough so that they can absorb the liquid. Any longer and they will crumble and fall apart.

4 Arrange a layer of sponge fingers in a shallow dish and cover them with the mascarpone. Continue making layers of sponge fingers, followed by mascarpone, ensuring that the topmost layer is of mascarpone.

5 Chill the tiramisu in the refrigerator for 3 – 4 hours, dust with cocoa powder and serve. I personally find tiramisu tastes better the following day, as the cheese absorbs the flavour of coffee as well.

You can vary the recipe a bit. If you do not want a coffee flavour, substitute orange juice or even mango juice—but in that case don't dust the tiramisu with cocoa powder, but decorate it with segments of oranges or sliced mango instead.

Showing off

Showing off

Cooking food for friends without any pressure is wonderful, but once in a while, I want to go all the way and make really unusual food which looks spectacular on the table. Food which will have my guests gaping, and giving me a standing ovation.

I experience a high every time I create a menu at Diva. I want to cook something exciting, something which looks better than it did on the last menu. Fresh shiitake mushrooms for vegetarians; beetroot adding colour to the gnocchi; gorgeous, shimmering strawberries covered with gold foil; little drops of balsamic vinegar adding body to the plate. Dinner has to be voluptuous, seductive and drop-dead gorgeous.

Most of us never give thought to cooking show-off food at home but the truth is that it takes very little to make a statement. All you do is vary the cuts: a whole roast chicken and a leg of lamb are no more difficult to cook than individual portions but they look very impressive when served on the table. Sugar strings to decorate cakes with are easy to make and everyone will think you've bought your homemade chocolate cake from a fancy patisserie. Often it is the ingredients that set apart a special meal—your guests will be impressed if you served pork, for example, a meat not usually cooked in Indian homes and no harder to prepare than mutton or chicken.

Some of this food does however take more effort to make. Making a crespelle takes practice, learning to cook with filo pastry can be tricky, the saffron risotto with prawns calls for making fish stock, and you will need to make pastry for Torta della nonna. But that's the point of this chapter. You've graduated from the easy stuff and it's time you tried your hand at something more challenging. Remember, you're showing off. Your meal can't just be about nourishment, it is about appeal—to the eye, the mouth and the insides. We are talking leather pants, high-heeled boots and painted nails.

Bagna cauda

Anchovy & olive oil dip | Piedmont

This Piedmontese starter literally means warm sauce, and that's exactly what it is. This dish is about community eating. A pot of bagna cauda is placed in the centre of the table and everyone dip their veggies in it. Again there are many recipes for it, but this is the one I love.

75 ml extra virgin olive oil
4 – 5 cloves garlic, peeled
  and minced
6 anchovies fillets preserved
  in olive oil, chopped
50 g unsalted butter, cut
  into chunks
Crushed black pepper
2 tbsp cream (optional)

FOR DIPPING
A variety of raw vegetables
  including fennel bulb,
  cauliflower, carrot,
  cucumber, red and yellow
  pepper, artichoke and
  zucchini, cut into ideal
  sizes for dipping

1 Sauté the crushed garlic and chopped anchovy fillets in the oil. Stir constantly until the anchovies disintegrate.

2 Add butter and mix. Add pepper to taste. I prefer the strong garlic taste but in case you want it milder, soak the cloves in milk for a few hours or add a small amount of cream at the last minute. This sauce is served in a pot, for everyone to dip the vegetables into, or in individual terra-cotta bowls.

Bagna cauda must be placed over warmers as it must simmer constantly. It is best made for a bigger party where people are going to help themselves, or as a snack for a winter evening. There is no salt in the recipe since anchovies are very salty, however adjust the seasoning as per your taste.

Cremino di barbabietole

Cream of beetroot & berries | Novarra

There is a quaint restaurant named Alla Torre in Romagnano Sesia in north Italy which serves the most amazing food. We were there during a grand trip to Piedmont to celebrate Gita's birthday, and for me the entire menu was pure poetry. This dazzling dish was a part of the eight course meal we had there.

1 kg beetroot
200 g strawberry or any berry
2 tbsp olive oil
1 tbsp rosemary
1 tbsp parsley, chopped
A few drops of balsamic vinegar
Salt & pepper to season

1 Preheat oven to 200°C.

2 Peel the beetroot and boil till tender, about 20 minutes. Slice the beetroot.

3 Mix olive oil, balsamic vinegar, rosemary, salt and pepper in a mixing bowl. Add the beetroot and mix well so it is evenly coated. Arrange on a baking tray and roast for about 20 minutes. Let it cool.

4 Blend the beetroot well with the berries in a food processor. Add a little water if you need, to obtain the consistency of single cream. Season and refrigerate.

5 Serve with a little sprinkling of chopped parsley.

I use this recipe very often for a large lunch party and serve it in little shot glasses as an appetiser. You could also serve it for summer lunch as a cold soup.

Uova sode al dragoncello

Stuffed eggs with tarragon | Tuscany

This antipasti comes from Siena, in Tuscany. I first tasted it as a part of a large antipasti platter with crusty bread, olives, marinated shrimps and cured meats. We had not ordered the eggs but were told that they were sent by the chef because he liked Indians. Lucky us, as these stuffed eggs are considered a delicacy. I love to make them for a big party as a part of a buffet, or even as canapés.

4 eggs
1 handful tarragon or
  parsley, finely chopped
20 ml extra virgin olive oil
2 tbsp canned tuna fish,
  drained
A few capers drained
  and chopped
Salt & pepper to taste

1 Place the eggs in a saucepan, and cover them with cold water. Bring the water to boil and let the eggs boil for 10 minutes. Remove them from the water, cool and peel the shells off.

2 Cut the eggs in 2 lengthwise, and gently remove the yolk. Put the yolk in a bowl with the herb, capers and tuna. Mash the mixture up with a fork till it becomes smooth. Season with salt and pepper.

3 Spoon the filling into the egg white shell, arrange on a plate and serve.

> You can vary the filling, and substitute the tuna with finely chopped spicy sausages or canned artichokes.

Crespelle con funghi

Mushroom pancakes | Florence

Crespelle are very thin pancakes rolled with a stuffing of your choice and baked with béchamel. The original crespelle comes from Florence and is rolled with spinach and ricotta.

FOR CRESPELLE
200 g white wheat flour
200 ml milk
2 eggs
200 ml water
20 g butter
Salt to season

FOR THE FILLING
400 g mushrooms, sliced
1 handful parsley, chopped
30 g Parmesan, grated
A bit of extra virgin olive oil
Salt to season
200 g béchamel (p 25)

1 First prepare the crespelle. Whisk the eggs with salt in a small bowl. Put the flour in a large bowl and slowly stir in the milk and the water at room temperature. Add the eggs and beat until smooth. Keep this mixture in the fridge for about 30 minutes.

2 Melt a very small piece of butter in a non-stick pan on high heat (you will do this only the first time when making crespelle). Using a medium-sized ladle, drop some of the mixture into the hot pan. Do not pour in too much as these pancakes have to be quite thin. Tilt the pan with a circular motion so that the batter coats the pan evenly. Cook each side until golden brown, about 2 minutes on each side. Remove and place on a plate. You'll need to practice this before you get the crespelle just right.

3 Preheat oven to 200°C.

4 Clean, trim and slice the mushrooms. Cook them for about 10 minutes in a pan with some extra virgin olive oil. Add a pinch of salt and cook for another 10 minutes. Sprinkle some parsley.

5 Place some of the mushroom mixture on each crespella and fold it into a triangle or roll it up like spring rolls. Make all the crespelle and line them in an oven tray. Cover with béchamel, which should have the consistency of a very fine, free-flowing cream. If the béchamel is too thick, it will coagulate after baking. Cover with Parmesan and dot with drops of butter. Bake in the oven for 20 minutes until golden brown. Serve warm.

> Because the crespelle itself is so subtle you can play with many variations of the stuffing. Mozzarella and ham, tomato and pesto, spinach and ricotta, crispy bacon and cheese being just some of them.

Cipolle arrosto con Parmigiana

Balsamic braised onions with Parmesan shavings | Umbria

This rustic dish has always been my last minute 'filler' every time I feel I need some more dishes on my buffet table, and I am out of time and ingredients. It was taught to me by Serra who used large red onions for it. However, I prefer to make it with baby onions. It is cooked on slow heat, which brings out the sweetness of the onion.

500 g baby onions or
  regular red onions, cut
  in quarters, with skin
100 ml vegetable or
  chicken stock
2 tbsp balsamic vinegar
A few sprigs of rosemary
50 ml red wine
1 tsp brown sugar
20 ml olive oil
Salt to taste
Parmesan for serving

1 Preheat the oven at 160°C.

2 Heat the oil in a large pan, add the onions and sauté on high flame for 2 – 3 minutes. Add the rest of the ingredients and cook for 5 minutes.

3 Transfer all the contents of the pan into a roasting tin. Bake in the oven for about 30 minutes.

4 In a platter, pile up the onions and serve with Parmesan shavings.

> I normally finish this in the oven, but you could continue to cook it in the pan, over very slow heat till the onions become soft. You could add pomegranate or feta cheese or just plain rocket leaves as topping.

Soufflé di piselli

Pea soufflé | Alto Adige

This Italian-style soufflé can be served as a starter or as a side dish. The best part about Italian soufflés is that, as they do not rise like the French soufflé, there is no risk of them deflating! This is a wonderful dish to make in winter with new season peas.

1 small onion, finely chopped
20 g butter
300 g fresh peas, shelled
100 g potatoes
40 g Parmesan, grated
2 eggs
20 ml olive oil
Salt & pepper to season

1 Preheat oven to 160°C.

2 Heat the oil and butter in a pan over medium heat. Sauté the minced onion, add the peas and a little bit of water. Cook till the peas are tender.

3 Meanwhile, boil the potatoes. When cooked, blend with the peas, Parmesan and eggs in a food processor. Season with salt and pepper. The mixture should be of the consistency of single cream.

4 Place the mix in individual buttered ramekins (small, cup-sized individual baking dishes) and bake for about 20 minutes.

5 The soufflé is done when a toothpick is inserted in the middle and it comes out clean. Serve immediately.

Torta di filo con spinaci, ricotta e zucca
Filo pie with spinach, ricotta & pumpkin | Tuscany

Filo is a wafer-thin pastry, widely used in Europe as well as the Middle East. The Italians normally refer to it as mille foglie, literally translated as thousand sheets due to its paper-like texture. You need to work very quickly with filo pastry, as it is very fragile and tends to dry very quickly. Readymade filo is easily available nowadays. (See p 218 for a list of suppliers.)

6 sheets filo pastry
200 g spinach, stems removed
200 g ricotta
200 g pumpkin, peeled
  and finely chopped
1 medium onion, chopped
50 g butter
1 pinch nutmeg
Salt & pepper to season
A bit of olive oil
1 tbsp white sesame seeds

1 Preheat oven to 200°C.

2 Blanch the spinach in boiling water for 5 minutes, then chop finely.

3 Heat the butter in a pan and sauté the onion till it turns pink. Add the pumpkin and sauté for another 6 – 8 minutes, till tender. Add the spinach and season with salt, pepper and nutmeg. Finally add the ricotta, and remove from the fire.

4 Next take a round cake tin. Brush each sheet of filo pastry with a bit of olive oil and place in the cake tin, each sheet slightly overlapping the other. So if your first sheet starts at the 12 o'clock hand, your next sheet could start at about quarter past, the next at half past, etc. The entire tin should be covered, with some amount of pastry hanging over the edges. Pour the spinach mixture in the centre, and cover it with the pastry that is hanging over the edges. It should now look like a bundle of filo, with the mixture inside it.

5 Brush the top with some oil, sprinkle with the sesame seeds and bake in the oven for about 20 minutes, or till golden brown.

> In case you are serving this dish for a sit-down dinner, you can make the same in smaller moulds and serve as individual main courses or starters. It is great eaten even the following day, just don't heat it in the micro-wave; you don't want it getting soggy. This is also a great dish for an outdoor lunch.

Tagliatelle con quattro formaggi e salsiccie

Tagliatelle with four cheeses & sausages | Trentino

This is one pasta which keeps making its way back onto the Diva menu every couple of years. Just when I think we have served it long enough and take it off the menu, I start getting requests for its return.

1 packet tagliatelle, boiled,
  plus a little pasta water
200 g pork sausages, fatty
  ones if possible, sliced
50 g mascarpone
75 g Gorgonzola
50 g Parmesan
50 g Fontina or Gruyére
1 handful parsley, chopped
2 tbsp butter
1 small onion, chopped
Salt & pepper to season

1 Heat the butter in a heavy saucepan, and sauté the onion till it turns pink. Add the sausages and increase the flame to high. Cook for about 5 – 6 minutes.

2 Add all the cheeses, except Parmesan, with a little bit of pasta water to make the consistency that of single cream.

3 Season with salt, pepper and parsley. Add the cooked pasta, sprinkle with Parmesan and serve.

Pasta con gremolata
Angel hair pasta with a citrus & parsley sauce | Umbria

The original recipe for this sauce uses lemon zest, garlic and parsley, a combination better known as gremolata in Italy. Gremolata is traditionally served with a great Italian veal stew called ossobucco but tastes wonderful with pasta as well. I have used orange rind instead of lemon, since it is difficult to find lemons in India and lime does not work too well here. Also, orange adds more colour to the pasta, which makes it look rather special. Don't underestimate this pasta because of its simplicity—the combination of orange and parsley is superb and elegant. It makes a wonderful summer first course.

2 oranges
3 cloves garlic, minced
1 handful parsley, chopped
1 packet angel hair,
  linguine or spaghetti
3 tbsp olive oil
50 g Parmesan, grated
Salt & pepper to taste

1 Grate the zest (peel) of the orange, being careful not to include the bitter white pith.

2 In a small bowl, mix the orange zest with garlic and parsley. Set the gremolata aside.

3 Cook the pasta in a large pot of boiling, salted water, following the directions on the packet.

4 Meanwhile, warm olive oil in a large pan over low heat, add the gremolata and season with salt and pepper. Cook for a minute.

5 Drain the pasta, and pour into the pan with a tablespoon of the pasta water. Stir well to mix the pasta with the gremolata. Sprinkle with Parmesan, garnish with a sprig of parsley and serve.

Involtini di maiale con Gorgonzola

Pork rolls with Gorgonzola & ham | Lombardy

Gorgonzola is a wonderful blue cheese from the Lombardy region in the north of Italy. I love using it as it gives a dish just the right amount of edge, yet is not as overpowering as other blue cheeses.

500 g pork loin
100 g cooked ham,
100 g Gorgonzola
1 handful thyme
2 tbsp extra virgin olive oil
Salt & black and green
  pepper to season

1 Cut the pork into about 8 slices. Beat the slices thin with a steak hammer. Or place them between 2 sheets of plastic wrap and beat them flat with a rolling pin. Sprinkle with salt, green pepper and black pepper. Throw some thyme leaves on the pork. Now place a slice of ham and some Gorgonzola on each slice and roll it up. Secure the involtini (roll) with a toothpick.

2 In a shallow pan, heat the oil and cook the involtinis until they are golden brown, say 5 – 7 minutes. Serve with vegetables of your choice.

> You could use bacon instead of ham, cooking the bacon before hand. Also sometimes I like to add a slice of pear as well. The slight sweetness of pear cuts the sharpness of the cheese.

Risotto con barbabietola e formaggio di capra

Beetroot & goat cheese risotto | Diva

This is currently my favourite dish at Diva. The combination of goat cheese and beetroot is a heady one, and the dish looks very pretty.

200 g Arborio rice
500 ml vegetable or chicken
  stock, or more if required
50 g butter
50 ml olive oil
1 medium onion, minced
1 medium beetroot, boiled
  and cut into small cubes
100 g goat cheese
100 ml white wine
Salt & pepper to taste
Grated Parmesan to serve

1 In a heavy saucepan melt half the butter with the olive oil over medium heat. Sauté the onion and beetroot for a minute or two. Add the rice and wine, let the rice be coated with the liquid, then start adding the stock, ladle by ladle. Continue the process for about 20 minutes or till rice is tender (p 6).

2 Add the goat cheese. The risotto will now get a creamy texture and a nice pink colour. Season with salt and pepper. Remove from heat, add the remaining butter and cover for 5 minutes.

3 Serve with grated Parmesan.

Risotto al mare
Risotto with prawns & saffron | Veneto

This is a fresh and aromatic risotto with a really sophisticated combination of flavours.

300 g medium prawns,
 deveined and cut into
 small pieces
100 g unsalted butter,
 divided into 3 parts
1 small yellow onion,
 finely chopped
2 cloves garlic, minced
200 g Arborio rice
100 ml dry white wine
 like Sauvignon Blanc
1 pinch saffron, soaked
 in warm water
1 handful parsley, chopped
50 ml heavy cream (optional)
500 ml fish or prawn stock
Salt & pepper to taste

1 In a heavy-bottomed saucepan, heat one third of the butter over medium-high heat. When the foaming subsides, add the prawns and cook till light pink for about 2 – 3 minutes. Remove the prawns from the pan and set aside.

2 In the same pan, add another third of the butter and sauté the onion until translucent. Add the garlic and cook a few minutes more. Add the rice, and stir until well-coated with the butter. Sauté lightly for a few moments, until the rice starts to turn translucent, then add the wine and stir constantly until evaporated.

3 Begin adding the stock by the ladleful (about ½ cup), stirring constantly until the rice is creamy and al dente, about 25 – 35 minutes. Always make sure there's enough liquid to cook the rice; it should bubble gently like old-fashioned oatmeal or what we call daliya. If it dries out or becomes clumpy, add more stock or water.

4 Add the saffron. Stir in the prawns, the remaining butter, parsley and heavy cream if you are using it. Season to taste with salt and pepper. Serve immediately.

> Normally cream is never added to risottos, but can be used in recipes which call for some delicacy and finesse, like this one. However feel free to not use the cream and just add a dollop of butter before serving.

Gamberoni alla salsa verde

Prawns in salsa verde | Cinque terre

Salsa verde literally means green sauce (salsa: sauce, verde: green). It is a piquant, zingy tasting sauce which works fabulously with all kinds of food. Serve it with just grilled chicken or fish. The sauce is usually made by combining olive oil, lemon juice, parsley and garlic. The southern version of this sauce also has capers in it. In this recipe, the prawns are cooked in the sauce.

1 kg prawns, deveined
  and cleaned
1 onion
2 stalks celery
1 large carrot
1 tbsp white wine vinegar
Juice of 2 limes
1 handful parsley
2 cloves garlic
½ cup olive oil
Salt & pepper

1 Put the prawns, onion, celery and carrot in a pan of boiling water. When the mix begins to boil again, add vinegar, lime juice and a pinch of salt. Cook for about 2 minutes.

2 Chop the parsley and garlic finely. With a wooden spoon, slowly beat in the olive oil. Season with salt and pepper.

3 Spread a bit of the green sauce on the platter on which you intend serving the prawns, pile on the prawns and drizzle with a little more sauce. Serve with wedges of lime.

Pesce in saor

Sweet & sour fish | Venice

This recipe comes from the romantic city of Venice and is normally eaten at Christmas time with soft polenta. My dear friend Giannina, who is first a Venetian and then an Italian, swears by this recipe. The pine nuts and the raisins are eastern influences, and Venice as the leading port of Italy during the Middle Ages and Renaissance was particularly open to different cultures. (The dome of St Marks is perhaps the most famous architectural example of the eastern influences in the city.) Historically, this dish was made in this way to preserve the fish. It is easy to make and the results are superb.

500 g onions, thinly sliced
2 tbsp olive oil
120 ml white wine vinegar
250 ml dry white wine
2 tbsp raisins or currants
2 tbsp pine nuts, toasted
2 bay leaves
1 kg white fish fillets
Salt to taste
Any good oil for frying fish

1 Fry the onions gently in the olive oil till very soft. Cover the pan to prevent the onions from browning too much. Add the vinegar, wine, raisins, pine nuts and bay leaves. Season with salt and pepper and simmer gently for about 15 minutes.

2 Cut the fish fillets into pieces about 5 cm long. Lightly salt and flour the fish, and fry quickly in batches, in hot vegetable oil, turning over once. Place on paper towels to drain.

3 Layer the fish in a serving dish and cover with the sauce. This dish is best eaten 1 – 2 days after making.

> Normally this dish is eaten at room temperature, but I like my food hot. In case you like it cold, you could serve it as an antipasti or as a cold main course on a summer day. Traditionally a winter dish served with polenta, this could also be served in summer with some pan-grilled vegetables or just a big green salad.

Sformato di pollo allo zafferano

Chicken mould with saffron sauce | Tuscany

Mrs Armellini, the other half of the Italian ambassador to India, gave me a collection of recipes contributed by members of the Italian Association of London. It truly is a delightful collection of home-style Italian recipes from north to south. I tried this one and was amazed by the results.

FOR THE MOULD
2 chicken breasts
4 eggs
200 ml single cream
30 g butter

FOR THE SAUCE
100 g carrots
200 ml chicken stock
1 pinch saffron
200 ml single cream
20 g butter
Salt & pepper to season

1 Preheat the oven to 200°C.

2 Cut the chicken into small pieces and place in a food processor. Add the cream, eggs and melted butter and blend till you get a liquid mixture. Pour the mixture into a ring mould or individual small moulds, place it on a dish of water (bain-marie, p 53) and bake for about 40 minutes.

3 Now make the sauce. Cut the carrots in small pieces and sauté in butter. Add the broth and the saffron. Cook for about 20 minutes, add cream and season with salt and pepper. Blend in the processor to get a thick sauce.

4 Take the chicken ring out of the mould and place on a platter. Spoon the sauce over it, garnish with sprigs of fresh basil and serve right away.

> This is a great dish for a big buffet or to prepare as individual servings for a second course. It has a very delicate flavour and should not be mixed with something very strong.

Petti di pollo al balsamico
Chicken breasts with balsamic vinegar | Emilia Romagna

Emilia Romagna lies in northeast Italy and is known as the 'food basket' of Italy. Parma ham, Parmesan and my most favourite ingredient—balsamic vinegar—come from this region.

4 chicken breasts
50 g all-purpose flour
50 ml extra virgin olive oil
1 medium onion,
  finely chopped
2 cloves garlic, minced
50 ml chicken stock
2 tbsp balsamic vinegar
1 handful basil
Salt & pepper to season

1 Beat the chicken breasts with a steak hammer to make thin piccatas. Alternately place each chicken breast between 2 sheets of plastic wrap and beat them with a rolling pin till they are quite flat. Dredge the chicken piccatas in the flour, shaking off any excess.

2 Heat the olive oil in a large pan over a high flame. Add the chicken in a single layer. Season with salt and pepper. Cook until golden on the bottom, about 2 minutes. Turn and cook the other side until golden, about another 2 minutes. Remove to a platter and cover with foil to keep warm.

3 Add the onion and garlic to the same pan and cook for about a minute. Add the chicken stock and reduce over high heat for a minute, scraping up any browned bits from the bottom of the pan.

4 Add the balsamic vinegar and cook until the sauce reduces and becomes syrupy, about a minute or 2. Stir in the basil, return the chicken to the pan, and turn a few times to coat with the sauce and to warm through. Serve hot.

> The same recipe will work with pork fillets and even with duck.

Pollo arrosto con melograno
Whole roasted chicken with lemon & pomegranate | Alto Adige

Whole roasts are easy to do and look spectacular on the table. This chicken looks particularly grand and colourful. You could also use the same recipe with a whole turkey or guinea fowl.

1 roasting chicken, about
  1½ kg, ask the butcher to
  remove the innards
Grated zest of 1 sweet lime
  (then cut sweet lime
  into quarters)
Grated zest of 1 orange
  (then cut orange
  into quarters)
100 g peeled and seeded
  pomegranate
Salt & pepper to season
50 ml olive oil
1 handful basil, shredded
4 tbsp fresh lime juice
100 ml white wine, like
  Chenin Blanc or
  Sauvignon Blanc
3 tbsp honey
Orange sections to garnish

1 Preheat the oven to 180°C.

2 Rub the outside of the chicken with one of the lime quarters, then discard.

3 In a small bowl, stir together the sweet lime and orange zests and half the lime juice. Rub this mixture evenly into the cavity. Put the lime and orange quarters along with pomegranate seeds and basil leaves inside the bird.

4 Place the chicken on a rack in a roasting pan. Sprinkle it with salt and pepper.

5 In a small bowl, combine the olive oil, remaining lime juice, honey and wine. Mix well.

6 Place the chicken in the oven and roast, basting with the dressing at least 4 times during cooking, until the juices run clear when the thigh is pierced with a knife, after about an hour.

7 Transfer to a serving platter and let rest for 10 – 15 minutes. Carve the chicken. Garnish with the orange sections and pomegranate seeds.

Agnello al presto
Very quick lamb chops | Marche

This recipe from the Marche region is really a very quick way of cooking mutton chops. It is also known as agnello scottaditto, which means burnt fingers. The good folks of Marche believe it is so delicious that no one can wait for it to cool down, resulting in burnt fingers! I recommend you use a fork and knife. And although this is a remarkably simple recipe, lamb or mutton chops aren't seen often at our tables and you'll impress everyone by cooking them, without too much effort. Served straight from the barbecue, this dish is great for an outdoor meal. You ought to tenderize the meat in papaya pulp as described on p 8.

12 lamb or mutton chops
2 cloves garlic, finely chopped
2 tbsp fresh rosemary, chopped
  or 1 tbsp dried rosemary
30 ml olive oil
A bit of bacon fat (optional)
Salt & pepper to taste

1 In a small bowl stir together the garlic, rosemary, olive oil, salt and pepper. Place the chops in a shallow dish and rub them with the marinade. Cover and refrigerate for at least 2 hours.

2 Start a fire in a charcoal grill or preheat a gas grill. Place the chops on the rack over high heat and grill, turning once, 5 minutes each side for medium rare. The outside will be well seared with the insides still pink. In case you want it cooked medium, cook for about 6 minutes on each side. You could also cook the chops in a pan on very high heat, in which case I recommend you add bacon fat to the marinade. You will need about 3 minutes on each side.

3 Transfer to a warm platter and serve immediately with a drizzle of olive oil.

> There are many ways in which you can vary this recipe. You could drizzle the chops with some balsamic vinegar, or even basic tomato sauce. To create another dish altogether, just top it with the mushroom sauce from pollo con funghi (p 57).

Cosciotto di agnello alle erbe

Roast mutton leg with herbs | Piedmont

A simple roast leg of mutton, if made well, can become the centrepiece of your table. Ask the butcher to prepare the leg the way he would prepare it for making raan. This cut is already very tender, but you must marinate it to ensure the meat will be really tender.

1 – 1½ kg leg of lamb
1 medium onion
1 handful mint
A few sprigs of rosemary
1 handful basil, torn
1 tbsp grainy mustard
1 tbsp bread crumbs
50 ml olive oil
50 ml white wine
2 cloves garlic, minced
Salt & pepper to season

1 Preheat oven to 200°C.

2 Make a paste of onion, garlic, bread crumbs and all the herbs with a little bit of olive oil in a food processor. Rub the paste all over the leg of lamb and let it sit for an hour or two.

3 Place the lamb in a roasting tray and season with salt and pepper. Drizzle with olive oil and sprinkle the wine over it.

4 Roast it in the oven for about 90 minutes, basting with the pan juices frequently.

5 Serve with greens and potatoes.

> About 45 minutes after putting the lamb in the oven, you could add some peeled whole baby onions and scrubbed baby potatoes to the roasting tray, and let these cook in the juices of the lamb.

Torta della nonna

Grandmother's cake | Originally from Tuscany

This is my weapon when I need forgiveness from someone. So far it has never failed me. Although traditionally a Tuscan cake, every Italian household has its own version. This one is my preferred recipe, from the south, where almond is used instead of pine nuts.

FOR THE PASTRY
175 g plain flour
75 g caster sugar
125 g normal butter, chilled
1 egg yolk
¼ tsp baking powder
Rind of 1 lime, finely grated

FOR THE FILLING
2 eggs whole
1 egg yolk
50 g caster sugar
4 tsp cornflour
200 ml milk
400 ml double cream

FOR THE GARNISH
Icing sugar, sifted
Toasted almond flakes

1 To make the pastry, sift the flour with baking powder on a cold surface, as it is easier to work with the dough. Add sugar and grated lime rind. Make a well in the centre and add the butter and egg yolk. Rub the butter and egg yolk into the flour using just your fingertips, until the flour attains a crumb-like texture. As you knead it further, it will start taking the shape of dough. Gather the dough together and roll it out to a round shape on a greased surface. This is your pastry.

2 Take a fluted tart mould, normally 8 or 9 inches in diameter, available easily. Press the pastry into the corners and up the sides of the mould. Trim the edges of the pastry with a knife and refrigerate for an hour.

3 Preheat oven to 200°C.

4 Take the pastry out of the fridge and prick the bottom of it with a fork, then line it with foil paper. Fill the pastry with any beans or lentils such as white channa or rajma, which will weigh pastry down while baking so that the pastry remains firm and does not puff up while baking. This also ensures you won't get a soggy raw crust when you bake the pastry with the custard. Place the pastry in the oven and bake for 15 minutes. The edges should be slightly brown.

5 For the filling, place the eggs, egg yolk, sugar, cornflour and lemon rind in a bowl and whisk well.

6 Heat the milk and cream together in a heavy based saucepan, but do not let it boil. If it boils, the filling is sure to curdle and you will have to start again. Take the milk off the heat and pour it into the egg mixture, whisking all the while.

7 Return to pan and cook over low heat, stirring constantly, till the mixture thickens. The consistency of the custard should be of a thick sauce or cream, still flowing, but not too liquid.

8 Pour the mixture into the pre-baked pastry case, and bake it in the oven again for 30 minutes, till the custard is set.

9 Serve the cake at room temperature, dusted with icing sugar and garnished with toasted almond flakes.

You are essentially making custard for the filling, which is made by adding beaten egg and sugar to hot milk and warming the mixture till it thickens. Custard has a tendency to curdle, so be careful. Make sure you cook the custard over low heat stirring continuously. The cornflour added to the eggs will also help stabilise them. Some people use a double boiler (a smaller dish set within a larger dish) to cook the custard, but I do not think this is necessary as long as it is cooked over slow heat.

Torta di cioccolato

Chocolate torta | Tuscany

This has been a Diva classic ever since we opened. It is terribly simple to make and the results are so impressive. The important ingredient is chocolate. It has to be the darkest you can get hold of.

250 g chocolate
125 g unsalted butter
3 eggs
50 g sugar
½ tbsp dark cocoa powder

1 Grease a 10-inch baking tin with some butter and line it with parchment paper.

2 Preheat oven to 200°C.

3 Break the chocolate into pieces and melt with butter in a double boiler (p 53).

4 Separate the eggs. In a bowl, beat the sugar with the egg yolks. Add the chocolate and butter mixture and the cocoa powder and mix well.

5 Beat the egg whites until stiff with a hand whipper or an electric beater, and fold them into the chocolate mix.

6 Pour the mix into the cake tin and bake for about 10 minutes. Lower the heat to 160°C and bake for another 35 minutes. Cool, unmould and serve, decorating with powdered sugar and caramel (as explained on the next page).

Decorating the cake

With some very simple techniques you can make any torta or dessert look gorgeous. Sifting icing sugar or cocoa powder over a dessert is the easiest and simplest way to make it look stunning.

Another garnish which can be made easily is caramel threads and sticks. Just melt some sugar in a pan till molten brown, let the caramel cool a bit, dip in a spoon and start pulling threads around your hand in a swift motion. For caramel sticks, place a piece of foil paper on a clean flat surface and grease it slightly with butter. Pour the caramel over in random shapes and let it cool. Remove when cool and stick it vertically into the cake or dessert so that it towers over the dish. Voila!

Cooking
for the
beloved

Cooking
for the beloved

How does one cook for love? I cook every day for my profession yet I am a bundle of nerves when I cook for my lover, and this has led to many disasters—including undercooked cakes and burnt pastry.

The erotic power of food has been celebrated and respected through the centuries. Casanova ate 50 oysters every morning. The Romans had a special fondness for figs and would consume them before frolicking in their bedrooms. Onions were forbidden to Egyptian priests as they might have made them feel too amorous.

Combining food with love, though, is not just about the aphrodisiac properties of food. It is about the enhancement of every sense. The food should look as good as it tastes, and then taste better than expected. Love-making, cooking and eating use the same senses—sight, smell, and touch. Play with flavours and textures of food; chilled avocado mousse followed by peppery prawns. Feel the tingling in your mouth with the two extreme flavours. The spices in the prawn will make your eyes water, your lips burn, awaken every sense in your body, and alert every inch of your skin. And then the sweetness of the sauce should provide relief.

All the recipes here are easy but sophisticated. Most can be prepared quickly or in advance. We do not want you getting all hot and sweaty, nor do we want you to be spending all your time behind the stove. I've also selected recipes using ingredients that are said to have aphrodisiacal qualities, with a particular emphasis on light food. We don't want you to go on a moonlit walk after dinner and collapse half way under the weight of your risotto. I hope these get you in the mood for love.

Mousse di avocato

Avocado mousse | Diva

I am not a 100 percent sure how Italian this recipe is, but I made it for President Ciampi in 2005 and he loved it. That makes it simple. If he loves it, it qualifies for this book. Avocado is considered a great aphrodisiac, and more importantly this is a delicate and light starter, which goes down very easily. A great beginning for the two of you!

600 g ready-to-eat avocados
10 g gelatin
50 ml milk
75 ml double cream, chilled
Salt & pepper to season

1 Cut the avocado, remove the seed and chop the flesh. Blend in a food processor till creamy.

2 Warm the milk and dissolve the gelatin in it.

3 Add the cream and milk to the avocado mixture. Mix well and season with salt and pepper.

4 Pour the mixture into slightly oiled ramekins or individual moulds, and refrigerate till set, about 3 – 4 hours.

5 Unmould and serve with Melba toast and a light drizzle of olive oil.

> Serve this dish very quickly after it is made, as avocado loses its beautiful colour very quickly. This dish is also very nice served with boiled prawns, with just a bit of olive oil and lime juice. For vegetarians, I sometimes decorate it with segments of orange, which enhance both the flavour and the colour.

Insalata di carciofi marinati
Marinated artichoke hearts | Calabria

They say in the 16th century only men were allowed to eat artichokes, as these were thought to enhance the sexual appetite. Marilyn Monroe was the first artichoke queen in 1949, at a beauty pageant held in California. For me, it is the whole ritual and the hands-on way of eating an artichoke that makes this dish so exciting. All you people living in cities like Bangalore and Mumbai, where it is easy to find fresh artichoke, make it your playmate. For those who will be using the canned/bottled ones do not fret—they taste just as good.

1 kg fresh artichoke hearts,
   tough outer stalks removed
   or 450 g artichoke hearts
   in oil or brine
2 bunches lettuce or
   rocket leaves
100 g cherry tomatoes
1 medium spring onion,
   finely chopped
30 ml olive oil
A few drops balsamic vinegar
1 tsp honey
1 handful basil
30 g Parmesan shavings
Salt & pepper to season

1 Prepare the marinade in a mixing bowl. Mix oil, honey and balsamic vinegar. Add the chopped onion and season with salt and pepper.

2 Boil the artichokes in salty water for approximately 30 minutes if you are using them fresh.

3 Place the artichoke (whichever version you are using) in the marinade for about 10 – 15 minutes.

4 To serve, prepare a platter with a bed of salad leaves, place the artichoke hearts over the leaves, throw in a few halved cherry tomatoes and drizzle with the marinade. As the final finishing touch, top with Parmesan shavings (shave the cheese with a potato peeler).

> If you are using whole artichoke hearts, place the marinade on the side. Pick out the tough leaves until you get to the soft heart. Pick a leaf at a time, dip in the marinade and eat.

Datteri con pancetta

Dates wrapped with bacon | Sardinia

This is a great starter, and can be made with minimum effort.

18 dried dates
9 slices bacon

1 Preheat oven to 200°C.

2 Fry the bacon in a pan till slightly brown, yet not very crispy.

3 Wrap each date in half a slice of bacon. Secure with a toothpick.

4 Bake in the oven for about 5 – 7 minutes till the bacon is crisp. Serve hot.

> If you have Parma ham handy, you could use that instead of bacon. Skip frying it in a pan, and put it straight in the oven and bake for about 5 minutes. For vegetarians, I normally slash the dates, creating a little pocket, and stuff it with a sharp cheese like Parmesan, Gorgonzola or even goat's cheese, warm them in the oven for a couple of minutes, and serve right away.

Insalata degli innomorati

Braised figs with Parma ham | Diva

These moist, braised figs with Parma ham are just fabulous, perfect for an intimate dinner.

4 ripe, ready-to-eat figs
10 g butter
100 g Parma ham, sliced
1 pinch thyme
A few drops balsamic vinegar
Salt & pepper to season
A few drops olive oil to drizzle

1 Heat the butter in a pan. Cut the figs in halves or quarters, depending on their size. Sauté the figs on a high flame for a minute.

2 Add the balsamic vinegar and thyme and season with salt and pepper.

3 To serve, place the figs in the centre of a platter, top with sliced Parma ham, drizzle with a bit of olive oil and crushed black pepper. Serve.

A vegetarian version can be made using mozzarella instead of Parma ham. Figs are seasonal fruit and in case you want to make this with dry figs, just hydrate them in warm water for an hour or so, before following the same method. However, I would recommend you make this dish with fresh figs, for it is not quite the same with dry ones.

Linguine con vodka e caviare

Linguine with vodka & caviar | Rome

Caviar is considered a great aphrodisiac. This is a luxurious pasta, so don't waste it on just anyone. Also, red caviar is cheaper than black, so you decide which one you prefer to use. Romans traditionally eat this after a night at the opera.

1 packet linguine, boiled
 to al dente
150 g leeks, thinly sliced
1 clove garlic, minced
100 ml vodka
100 g sour cream
50 ml olive oil
50 g black or red caviar
Salt & pepper to season

1 Heat the oil in a pan and sauté the garlic and leeks. Cook for about 5 minutes.

2 Add the vodka and sour cream and cook over very low heat for 7 – 8 minutes.

3 Take it off from the fire, add the pasta and finally the caviar. Save a little bit of caviar to garnish. Season with salt and pepper.

> Make sure you add the caviar just before serving, you do not want the caviar to get overcooked.

Spaghetti al cartoccio
Spaghetti with seafood in paper parcel | Cinqueterre

This dish calls for a little bit of work while you are assembling it, but looks incredible when presented on the table. It is best presented individually and is perfect for a sit-down meal. I have used prawns and mussels, but you can use any seafood you like. Make this with just prawns, or even fish and adjust the quantity accordingly; change the quantity to 350 grams if you are using only one kind of seafood.

1 packet spaghetti or
  linguine, boiled, plus a
  little cooking water
300 g mussels
200 g prawns, deveined
  and peeled
75 ml olive oil
100 ml dry white wine,
  like Sauvignon Blanc
300 g basic tomato sauce (p 27)
2 cloves garlic, minced
1 handful basil
1 handful parsley, chopped
Parchment paper or
  aluminium foil

1 Preheat oven to 150°C.

2 Scrub the mussels well under running water, and cut off the 'beard' with a sharp knife. The beard refers to the bunch of fibre-like threads mussels have. They need to be cut before cooking. Also mussels tend to be very sandy so make sure you wash them thoroughly under cold running water to get rid of all the grit.

3 Sauté the garlic in a deep saucepan. Add the mussels and wine. Increase the heat till the mussels open up. Discard the ones that do not open. Remove the mussels from the saucepan and set aside.

4 Bring the saucepan back to the fire and sauté the prawns in the same liquid. Once the prawns are cooked, add the basic tomato sauce, and the open mussels. Add parsley and basil and season with salt. Add the boiled spaghetti with a little bit of pasta water. Toss well.

5 Prepare 4 pieces of parchment paper or aluminum foil, say about 12 x 16 inches.

6 Place each sheet in the centre of a shallow bowl. Place a mound of pasta in the centre of each hollow, and twist the ends together to close the packet. Arrange in a large baking tray, and bake in the oven for 7 – 8 minutes.

7 Place each packet on an individual plate, and open it on the table.

Sformato di funghi misti

Mushroom flan | Lombardy

Sformato is a sort of Italian baked custard or flan. Normally it is served as a first course in Italy, but I serve it as a main course for vegetarians. Mushrooms are meant to be aphrodisiacs.

150 g béchamel (p 25)
500 g mushroom, sliced
50 ml olive oil
1 small onion, finely chopped
1 pinch ground nutmeg
50 g Parmesan, grated
2 whole eggs
2 egg yolks
50 g butter
50 g bread crumbs,
  lightly toasted

FOR THE FONDANT (SAUCE)
100 g Fontina or Gruyére
  cheese, grated
100 g heavy cream
Salt & pepper to taste

1 Preheat oven to 200°C.

2 In a pan, heat the olive oil and sauté the onion and mushroom till brown.

3 Let it cool, then purée half the mushroom mix in a food processor till smooth and creamy.

4 In a mixing bowl, mix the puréed mushroom with the béchamel, salt, nutmeg, Parmesan, eggs and egg yolks. Stir until thoroughly combined. Gently fold in the remaining mushroom.

5 Butter a mould or individual small moulds and coat with bread crumbs. Fill the mould with the mushroom mix. Place it in a dish of water (bain-marie, p 53).

6 Bake until the top of the sformato is golden brown and a toothpick inserted into the centre comes out clean, about 35 to 40 minutes. Remove and allow to cool for 15 minutes.

7 Meanwhile, to make the sauce, mix the grated Fontina, heavy cream and the salt and pepper in a small sauce-pan. Heat gently, stirring constantly, until smooth and creamy.

8 To serve: turn the sformato out onto a large plate. Cut into 2-inch slices and place the slices on serving plates. Spoon the fondant over the slices and serve immediately.

Torta di asparagi

Asparagus tart | Liguria

This delicious tart from Liguria was always on the menu for my father whenever he visited my friend Serra, since as a strict vegetarian, he would not even eat eggs. But for me it works brilliantly when I am cooking a meal for seduction—easy to make, looks fantastic and asparagus is the perfect ingredient to get the romance going. This can be eaten as a first course or as an elegant main course for vegetarians.

FOR THE DOUGH

200 g flour, plus extra if needed
30 ml extra virgin olive oil, plus extra for greasing the pan
50 ml full fat milk, plus extra if needed
A pinch of salt

FOR THE FILLING

1 kg asparagus, trimmed and rough stalks removed
40 ml extra virgin olive oil
50 g Parmesan, grated

1 To make the dough, combine the flour, salt, milk and olive oil on a clean, flat surface. It's always easier to make the dough on a surface rather than in a bowl. Add a little more milk if the dough is dry, or a little more flour if the dough is sticky. Knead until smooth, and wrap in cling wrap. Let the dough rest at room temperature for an hour.

2 Preheat oven to 180°C.

3 Grease a round 12 or 16-inch pan, with low sides.

4 Meanwhile make the filling. In abundant salted boiling water, cook the asparagus for about 6 – 7 minutes, or until soft. Drain, plunge the asparagus in iced water and immediately remove it. This is so that the asparagus retains its bite. Drain again and blot dry. Chop finely.

5 Heat the olive oil in a pan over a medium heat. Add the asparagus, season with salt and sauté for 5 minutes. Cool to room temperature, fold in the grated Parmesan and adjust the salt if needed.

6 Roll out the dough until it is very thin on a lightly floured counter (it should measure about 20 inches, a few inches more than the base pan). Line the greased baking pan with the dough, letting excess dough hang over the sides of the pan. Spoon in the asparagus filling. Use the overhanging dough to create a pretty border around the tart.

7 Bake the tart in the preheated oven until the crust is golden, about 30 minutes. Serve hot, warm, or at room temperature.

Pesce agli agrumi
Fish with citrus marinade | Naples

This is a dish I have been making for years now, sometimes with sweet lime, sometimes with oranges or grapefruit, and sometimes with all three. Like most of the Italian fish recipes, this one too is breathtakingly simple. It looks stunning garnished with all the citrus. The Neopolitan style of cooking is like the people of the area, robust and colourful. They are particularly known for their use of citrus in the cooking, as the region is famous for its lemons.

1 kg fish fillet of your choice
50 ml extra virgin olive oil
75 ml white wine
50 ml freshly squeezed sweet
  lime or orange juice
Juice of 1 lime
1 handful oregano
2 oranges, or any other citrus
  fruit, sliced
Salt & pepper to season

1 In a mixing bowl, add the olive oil, wine, orange juice and lime juice. Add oregano, salt and pepper. Place the fish fillet in the marinade and give it a good shake.

2 Add the sliced fruits gently, as you'd like to keep them whole and not break into pieces. Cover the bowl and leave it in the fridge for an hour.

3 Heat a bit of oil in a non-stick pan and grill the marinated fillets, basting both sides with the marinade. Once the fish is cooked, remove and set aside.

4 In the same pan, on a high flame, cook the marinade for about 5 minutes to reduce the sauce. Pour over the fish and serve it garnished, with sliced fruits.

> I like to serve sautéed spinach with this fish, as the colours of spinach and orange contrast very prettily.

Gamberoni con pepe nero

Prawns with black pepper & oregano | Molise

This dish is really fun to eat with your lover. Here you are playing with flavours—the heat of black pepper and the sweetness of honey. The best way to cook this dish is to leave the shells on the prawns.

500 g prawns with the shell
  on (preferably not too large)
2 tbsp butter
50 ml olive oil
4 cloves garlic, chopped
1 fistful oregano, or 1 pinch
  dried oregano
100 ml dry white wine
1 tsp honey
Crusty bread

1 Clean the prawns, leaving the shells on. Devein them by pulling off the head and pulling out the black, thread-like intestine with the tip of a knife. Wash them under running water. Pat dry.

2 In a large frying pan, melt the butter with olive oil over medium heat. Add garlic, oregano and pepper, then immediately stir in the prawns. Cook, tossing for about 30 seconds.

3 Add white wine and honey, and cook for another 2 – 3 minutes.

4 Serve right away, accompanied by bread to mop up the juices, each diner peeling his or her prawn shells.

Insalata di arragosta

Warm lobster salad | Liguria

In India we get crayfish and not lobster. The difference is that our so-called lobsters do not have claws. They are like giant prawns, and the meat is in the tail portion. If you overlook this, the truth remains that shellfish really is one of the most romantic of foods. Lobsters' aphrodisiac history can be traced back to the ancient Greeks, who believed their goddess of love, Aphrodite, was born of the sea and that all ocean creatures were her playthings in the games of love.

1 lobster, weighing about 1 kg
50 ml extra virgin olive oil
Juice of 2 limes
1 handful basil, shredded
A pinch of chilli flakes
½ tsp honey
Salt & pepper to season
Salad leaves (I prefer rocket)

1 In a large, deep pan bring water to boil. Place the whole lobster in the pan and bring it to boil for about 8 – 9 minutes. The general rule is 7 minutes for every half kilo, but we do not want this fully cooked as there is a second process involved.

2 Remove the lobster from the water and let it cool. Make a slit with a sharp knife in the tail area of the lobster to remove the flesh.

3 Chop the lobster meat into manageable size of about 2-inch pieces.

4 In a mixing bowl mix oil, lime juice, basil leaves, chill and honey. Give it a good whisk, season with salt and pepper. Pour the dressing over the lobster meat and let it sit for about an hour.

5 Just before serving, toss the lobster with the dressing in a non-stick pan for about 3 – 4 minutes, on medium heat.

6 In a plate pile up the warm lobster meat, top it with salad leaves, and pour whatever liquid is in the pan as a dressing around the plate. Serve right away.

Pollo al sesame
Chicken with sesame crust | Sardinia

This recipe calls for a little bit of work but is worth the effort. A recipe from Sardinia, it is made with veal, but I have modified it and used chicken. At Diva I once made red snapper with a sesame crust and that, too, worked beautifully.

1 kg chicken breast
1 tsp garlic paste
50 ml olive oil
1 handful parsley, chopped
A splash of white wine
100 g white sesame seeds
1 egg white
Salt & pepper to season
Oil for shallow frying

TO SERVE
Eggplant purée (p 169)

1 Prepare the marinade in a mixing bowl. Add the oil, garlic paste, parsley and white wine. Season with salt and pepper.

2 Place the chicken breasts between 2 sheets of plastic wrap and beat with a steak hammer or rolling pin to flatten them a bit.

3 Add the chicken to the marinade and mix well. Let it sit for a couple of hours.

4 Take the chicken out from the marinade, and place it on a clean working surface. Brush the chicken pieces with egg white and coat with sesame seeds on both sides.

5 Heat the oil in a shallow pan. Fry on medium heat till the sesame seeds are golden in colour and the chicken is cooked. Slice and serve with eggplant purée or just some green salad.

You have to ensure the oil is not too hot, otherwise the chicken will remain raw from inside, and the sesame will burn. Another option is to bake it in a preheated 200°C oven with a few drops of butter or olive oil on the chicken. I prefer it fried.

Filetto di maiale con capperi

Pork fillet with capers | Umbria

This Umbrian way of cooking pork is delicious as they have fantastic meat and you can really taste the succulence of pork in this simple dish. It's important to use very good quality meat and fortunately we get fantastic quality pork in India. (See p 218 for a list of suppliers.) I recommend you use pork loin, which is the backside of pork, for the fillet—it is very tender.

500 g pork fillet
50 ml olive oil
Juice of 1 lime
1 tbsp capers, finely chopped
200 ml dry white wine
Salt & pepper to season

1 Cut the pork fillet in thin slices, cover in cling wrap, and beat with a steak hammer or rolling pin to make nice, thin fillets or piccatas.

2 In a shallow non-stick pan, heat the oil till it is very, very hot, add the meat and cook on both sides for 3 minutes, until brown.

3 Add the wine, lime juice, salt and pepper, cover the pan and cook again on very slow heat, for about 2 minutes. Sprinkle the meat with capers and continue to cook for another 1 – 2 minutes.

4 Serve on a warm plate with some mashed potatoes or grilled vegetables.

Pesche al vino rosso
Peaches poached in red wine

For me, peaches are the most perfect fruit in the world. I love their aroma, texture and colour. God definitely created them when he had loads of time on his hands. Also known to be a great aphrodisiac, peaches are a great way to end to an intimate dinner.

4 just-ripe peaches
50 g butter
100 ml red wine
50 g sugar
A sprinkling of cinnamon

1 Preheat oven to 200°C.

2 Slice the peaches in half and scoop out the seed.

3 In a shallow pan melt the butter, add all the ingredients and place the peaches on top. Let them simmer for a few minutes on very low heat, for about 20 – 25 minutes, till the peaches are tender.

4 To serve, remove the peaches from the pan and place on a warm plate.

5 Cook the liquid once again on a very high flame, for 2 minutes. Pour the sauce over the peaches and serve with either whipped cream or a scoop of vanilla ice cream.

Fragole con mascarpone

Marinated strawberries with mascarpone | Emilia Romagna

One really needn't say why this dish is featured in this chapter. Strawberries are a timeless classic to be served to your lover. However, marinating them in red wine gives them a slight twist, and eating them with mascarpone or cream, takes this simple fruit to another level altogether.

300 g fresh strawberries
100 ml red wine
75 g sugar
1 handful mint

Halve the strawberries and place them in a bowl. Sprinkle the sugar over them and cover with wine. Throw in the mint leaves. Mix well and let the strawberries marinade for at least 4 – 5 hours. I would even recommend that you leave it overnight. Serve with unsweetened cream or a dollop of mascarpone.

> Once in a while I marinate the strawberries in a few drops of balsamic vinegar or just a glass of orange juice instead of wine, which tastes just as good. Of course, if you want to go another step forward where romance is concerned, marinate them in champagne!

Pana cotta

Cream custard | Piedmont

Literally translated as cooked cream, pana cotta is one of the most sensual and delicious desserts in the Italian repertoire. It hails from Piedmont, north of Italy, where milk and cream is especially fatty. This is the one dessert which has never been off my menus, right from MezzaLuna till Diva. Recently though, pana cotta has given me some grief. On a recent trip to Piedmont to celebrate Gita's 50th birthday, our friends and family told me that my pana cotta was good, but nothing compared to the one at Antico Agnello at Lago D'orta, a wonderful restaurant where we once had a meal. So much for diplomacy!

500 ml full cream
100 g sugar
1 stick fresh vanilla or a few
  drops vanilla essence
½ tsp gelatin, dissolved in
  warm water

1 In a heavy saucepan, heat the cream over low heat. Add the sugar and cook for another 5 minutes.

2 Break the vanilla stick into pieces, add to the cream and cook for another 2 – 3 minutes.

3 Remove the cream from the flame, add the gelatin and stir to make sure the gelatin is fully dissolved. Give the mixture a good whisk.

4 Pour the pana cotta into small moulds. Sometimes I like to set it in martini or shot glasses. Place in the refrigerator overnight.

5 Unmould and serve with a topping of your choice. (See next page for toppings.)

Toppings

Here are some ideas for toppings. Choose what works best for you.

Mango sauce

Flesh of 1 mango, chopped
20 g sugar
1 tsp lemon juice
½ tsp butter

Sauté the mango in butter over a low flame. Add sugar and lemon. Purée to a fine sauce, adjusting the consistency with water if required, and pour over the pana cotta.

Strawberries & balsamic sauce

2 baskets strawberries,
 thinly sliced
2 tbsp balsamic vinegar
20 g sugar
Black pepper

Toss the strawberries with the balsamic vinegar, sugar and pepper in a large bowl. Let the mixture stand for at least an hour, tossing occasionally. Spoon over the pana cotta, not forgetting the juices, and serve.

Caramel & coffee topping

100 g sugar
50 g butter
50 ml double cream
1 tsp granulated instant coffee

1 Heat sugar on high heat in a heavy-bottomed saucepan. It is important that your pan has a heavy bottom, or else the sugar will burn. As the sugar begins to melt, stir constantly with a whisk. If you find the sugar burning, add a bit of water right away. As soon as all of the sugar crystals have melted (the liquid sugar should be dark amber in colour), immediately add the butter to the pan. Continue to whisk vigorously until the butter has melted.

2 Take the pan off the heat, add the coffee and give it another whisk. Add the cream to the pan and continue to whisk. When you add the butter and cream, the mixture will foam up considerably. Let it cool and settle down—you are now ready to spoon it over the pana cotta.

140

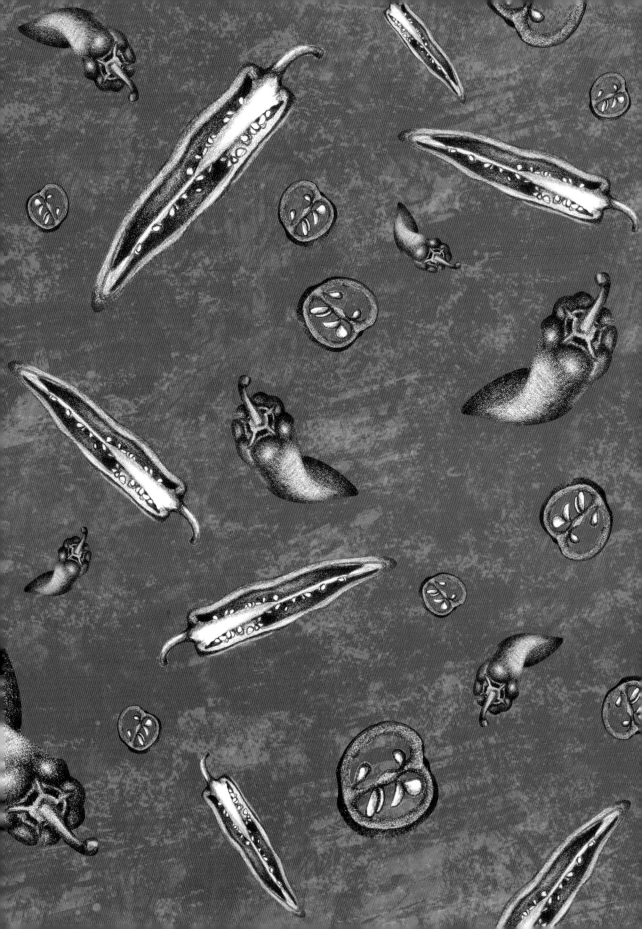

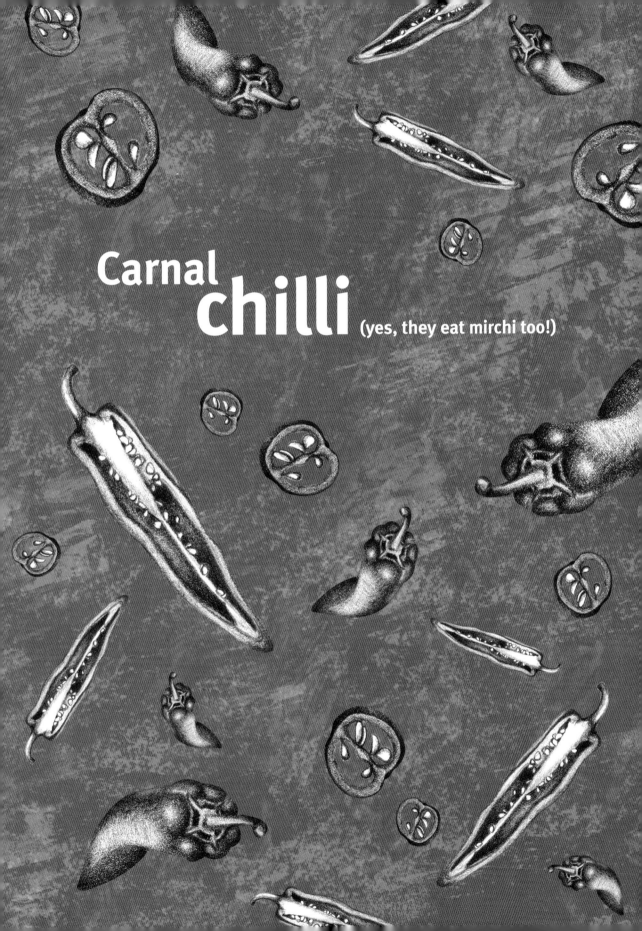

Carnal chilli

(yes, they eat mirchi too!)

Carnal chilli (yes, they eat mirchi too!)

Are you surprised? Well don't be, because the Italians, especially in the south, have great respect for their peperoncino. They use chilli rather differently from the way we do—it's used mostly just to add a bit of oomph to the dish so the heat will be very subtle. But what it does mean is that we Indians can happily go into an Italian restaurant, ask for chilli flakes and get it. The Italians might not approve of just how much and on what you use it, but it won't be denied to you.

All over Italy you will find chillies being used in stews, pasta, even in soups. You will find chillies in the basic tomato sauce in this book, in flavourings for fish, meats and even for vegetables. It has also been used as a preserving agent for meats like salami and pancetta, and often shows up on the table as a part of antipasti. In the south, oil flavoured with chillies, known as olio santo, is a very common condiment used at the drop of a hat. In fact in Calabria they even have a yearly peperoncino festival. I recently discovered that chillies in Italy are threaded by their stalks on a string and hung all over the house, particularly on front doors to keep the devil away. This practice is known as diavolicchio and refers to the heat associated with the devil.

Italian cooking uses two main varieties of chilli. Adorno is small, violet red and very hot. The other, Cilleghia piccante, looks like a little cherry tomato, and is very mild. It can be used as stuffing, or with pasta, and you will find it in all markets in Italy. I recommend you use the Kashmiri deghi mirch as a substitute where dried chilli is required. Use the larger variety of fresh red chillies when the recipe calls for fresh chilli. However, always keep one thing in mind when using peperoncino in Italian cooking—don't go overboard. You need to use chilli, when cooking Italian, with balance and moderation.

144

Sicilian fuoco

Hot pepper sauce | Sicily

This wonderful sauce must have been created with the thought that one day Indians would eat Italian food. Fuoco sauce can be kept for a long time in airtight containers, even up to a year. I use it to flavour almost everything. Anna, my Sicilian friend and mentor, always has millions of jars ready to give out as handy presents, and I believe one jar always goes in her Christmas hamper.

2 kg tomatoes, peeled,
   deseeded and chopped
500 g fresh red chilli, washed
   and stemmed
500 g capers, washed
3 cloves garlic
600 ml olive oil
1 bunch basil, torn
Salt & pepper to season

1 Place the roughly chopped tomatoes in a colander, sprinkle with salt and sugar and let all the juices drain for about 2 – 3 hours.

2 In a mixing bowl, mix the chilli with capers, garlic, basil and salt. Process in a blender with 100 ml olive oil only till the mix is coarsely chopped. You do not want a fine purée here.

3 Mix the tomatoes in batches into the sauce and again process in the blender till it reaches a fine consistency.

4 Transfer to a clean dry bowl and slowly add the remaining olive oil. Spoon the sauce into sterilised jars, cover and store in a cool dry place for at least 10 days before eating.

> You could use fuoco as a topping for bruschetta, dressing for fish, dip, seasoning for frittata, or even as part of a marinade.

Gita's penne arrabiata
Gita's enraged pasta | Calabria

This Calabrian dish is nearly as famous as Uncle Mac in my opinion. Every Indian who has a penchant for Italian will most likely start his or her journey with this pasta. It has never been on a Diva menu, yet I think we make at least 10 portions of it every night on request. I think I do a mean arrabiata, but someone who does it better than me is Gita—if you don't believe me ask the Bhalla clan.

500 g penne
2 onions, chopped
50 ml olive oil
3 cloves garlic, chopped
75 g Parmesan, grated
2 small fresh red chillies,
  deseeded and finely chopped
1 kg tomatoes, blanched,
  skinned and seeded
A pinch of sugar
Salt to season

1 In a pan heat the olive oil and cook the onion, garlic and chillies. Cook till the onions are brown. Add the tomatoes. Season with salt and sugar and let the mixture cook for about 15 minutes on low heat.

2 Meanwhile cook the pasta in salted water till al dente, reserving some of the pasta cooking water.

3 Mix the pasta with the sauce and half the Parmesan, and a bit of pasta water to give it a smooth consistency. Serve with the rest of the Parmesan cheese.

Spaghetti aglio olio e peperoncino

Spaghetti with oil, garlic & red chilli flakes | Naples

There is no pasta simpler than this one, and it can be put together in a matter of minutes. It is without any pretension, inexpensive and very, very satisfying. You can make it both with chilli, and without.

1 packet spaghetti
2 cloves garlic
50 ml extra virgin olive oil
1 handful parsley, chopped
1 large dried red chilli, or
   crushed red chilli flakes
Salt to taste

While the pasta is boiling, place the garlic, oil and chilli in a pan over medium heat. As soon as the garlic turns golden and you can smell its aroma, switch off the heat, add the chopped parsley, the cooked pasta, and just a little bit of pasta water. Toss well and serve right away.

Italians do not like the taste of garlic pieces, and use garlic only to perfume this pasta. However, we Indians love our garlic and if you prefer you can use chopped garlic, rather than whole cloves. This will give it a far more intense flavour, rather than that classic, subtle flavour that is so quintessentially Italian.

Spaghetti puttanesca

Whore's pasta | Naples

This famous pasta originates in Naples and literally means 'a whore's pasta'. This could be because of the spice in it, or because it is so easy to make that the busy tarts of Naples could prepare it between customers. Or it could be that these ladies had no time for shopping and this pasta doesn't require fresh vegetables. Whatever the etymology, Indians seem to love it. It works very well with our palate.

1 packet spaghetti (or penne), boiled
50 ml olive oil
1 handful parsley, finely chopped
200 g basic tomato sauce (p 27), or 1 can whole tomatoes, with juice
4 flat anchovy fillets, drained and minced (optional)
2 tbsp Mediterranean-style, brine-cured black olives, minced
2 tsp bottled capers, drained
2 cloves garlic, minced
½ tsp dried red chilli flakes
Salt to taste
Grated Parmesan for topping

1 Heat the oil in a saucepan and cook the garlic and the red chilli flakes over moderately low heat, stirring all the while. Stir in the parsley, and cook the mixture for 10 seconds.

2 Add the tomatoes with the juice or basic tomato sauce, and cook the mixture over moderate heat for about a minute.

3 Add the anchovies, the olives and capers and cook the sauce, stirring, for 2 minutes. Season with salt.

4 Toss the sauce with the cooked pasta and serve with lots of grated Parmesan.

This is a pasta which can be cooked within minutes. I prefer to make it with basic tomato and basil sauce, and I always have some sauce frozen for last minute cooking. But as I have suggested, you can use canned, peeled tomatoes, which are easily available now. The traditional recipe calls for anchovies and they definitely add oomph to the pasta, but you could very well do without.

Pasta alla kingfish
Pasta with kingfish | New Delhi

Gianna Gastaldi has always liked making this pasta for her Indian guests, since the chilli in the pasta suits their taste buds. She uses kingfish because it most closely resembles her favourite, swordfish.

350 g penne, fusilli or spaghetti
2 1 cm-thick slices kingfish,
  about 250 g, cut in small cubes
100 g cherry tomatoes, halved
2 cloves garlic, peeled
5 tbsp extra virgin olive oil
20 g fresh mint and basil,
  chopped
Minced red chillies to taste
Salt to taste

1 In a saucepan heat the olive oil over a medium flame, add garlic and cook for a minute. Add kingfish, season with salt and red chilli and stir well, cooking till the fish is done, about 4 minutes. Add the cherry tomatoes and after a minute, remove the pan from the heat.

2 Meanwhile bring 3 litres of salted water to a boil, add the pasta and cook until al dente.

3 Drain the pasta and put it into the pan with the fish sauce. Return to a medium-high flame and toss for a minute.

4 Place the pasta in a serving plate, sprinkle with mint and basil, and serve.

You could make this recipe as a fish dish by itself. Just prepare the fish as described, but don't cut the fish into pieces. Cook it as a whole steak or a fillet. It's very nice served with some baby potatoes.

Pesce alla Paula

Paula's fish | New Delhi

This is a simple dish that my friend Paula made when she tried going on a fish diet and wanted to cook something with a little bit more oomph. A 'quickie' with very satisfying results.

1 kg fillet of bekti, or any firm
  fish of your choice
3 cloves garlic, chopped
1 fresh red chilli, deseeded
  and chopped
40 ml olive oil
2 tbsp semolina—our good
  old suji
Salt & pepper to season

1 In a bowl mix the oil, chilli, garlic and seasoning. Coat the fish on both sides with the chilli oil. Cover the fish thoroughly with semolina.

2 In a non-stick pan, cook the fish for about 5 minutes on each side till it is cooked and the semolina coating is crisp on the outside. Serve with a wedge of lemon or lime.

> In case you have any chilli oil left, drizzle a bit over the fish before serving.

Mrs Bacchetti's pollo alla cacciatore

Hunter-style chicken | Puglia

I feel very sentimental about this classic dish. When Diva had just opened, every client was very, very precious. In those days, Gita was helping out at the restaurant. One day a family walked in. They ordered drinks, and began to examine the menu. That's when it all started to go pear-shaped; they thought this new 'Divya' restaurant would be serving Mughlai food. We couldn't afford to let any of our customers go as we were so short of them, so in desperation Gita told them I would cook them a dish that they would like, and that if they didn't it would be on the house. I made cacciatore for them, using the recipe given to me by Mrs Bacchetti, my friend Sabrina's mother. I am proud to say it was the family's first Italian dining experience, and seven years on I still see them at Diva, every couple of months, asking for cacciatore.

1 kg young chicken
1 medium onion, sliced
2 cloves garlic, crushed
  (but left whole)
½ cup virgin olive oil
40 g butter
Salt
½ cup dry white wine
  like Sauvignon Blanc

FOR THE SAUCE
1 onion, chopped
Chopped rosemary leaves
½ cup virgin olive oil
300 g red tomatoes, seeded
  and roughly chopped
Chilli powder to taste
40 g butter

1 Preheat oven to 200°C.

2 Cut the chicken into small pieces, rinse and dry. Put the chicken in a pan with the onion, garlic, oil, butter and a little bit of salt. When the garlic is a bit brown, take it out and discard it. When the chicken is browned, pour the wine over it.

3 Separately, in a small casserole, sauté the onion and rosemary in hot oil. When the onion starts to colour, add the tomatoes. Add some salt to taste and the chilli powder. Leave on a low fire for 20 minutes, then add the tomato-rosemary sauce to the chicken with some butter, if you like.

4 Put the chicken in a baking dish and bake in a hot oven for 20 minutes.

> If you like you can add fresh, sliced peppers (green, yellow or red), after you have poured the wine, and before you add the tomato-rosemary sauce.

Pollo alla diavola

Angel with two horns | Naples

This chicken looks as tame as an angel until you take a bite. There are many variations to this recipe everywhere in Italy, but this particular one is from Naples.

1 whole chicken, cut into
   8 pieces
50 ml olive oil
Juice of 2 limes
3 red chillies, crumbled
1 handful fresh oregano,
   or 1 tbsp dried oregano
100 ml any white wine
4 cloves garlic, minced

1 In a mixing bowl prepare the marinade. Add the olive oil, half the lime juice, wine, garlic, chilli and oregano. Add the chicken and let it sit in the marinade for a couple of hours.

2 Preheat oven to 180°C.

3 Heat some olive oil in a heavy pan, on a high flame. Add the chicken and let it brown on all sides, for 6 – 8 minutes.

4 Transfer the chicken to a roasting tray, pouring the marinade over it. Roast for about 30 minutes. Serve with the juices from the tray and a drizzle of the remaining lime juice.

Arista di maiale

Pork roulade | Tuscany

This is a fabulous Tuscan recipe for a simple pork roast and is served all over the Tuscan countryside. There are many variations to this recipe. Here I have covered it with bacon, but you don't have to. Some also like it lined with ham.

1 kg loin of pork, bone
  removed
Enough bacon to wrap
  around the roast
2 tbsp fennel seeds
2 tbsp olive oil
3 dried red chillies
8 cloves garlic
200 ml white wine
Rosemary, parsley and
  fresh herbs of your choice
Salt & pepper to season

1 Preheat oven to 180°C.

2 Rub salt and pepper into the pork loin.

3 Pound the garlic, fennel seeds and chilli into a paste. Rub the paste all over the meat. Sprinkle with fresh herbs. Wrap the roast in bacon and roll. Tie it with string and secure it. It should resemble a very fat salami.

4 Heat the oil in a roasting tray on the stove, and brown the roast on all sides.

5 Pour the wine into the tray, and place the roast in the pre-heated oven. Roast for 45 minutes, then reduce the temperature to 140°C and roast for a further 30 minutes. Take the roast out of the oven, leave it to stand, covered, for a few minutes. Remove the string, cut the meat into slices, and serve with the juices.

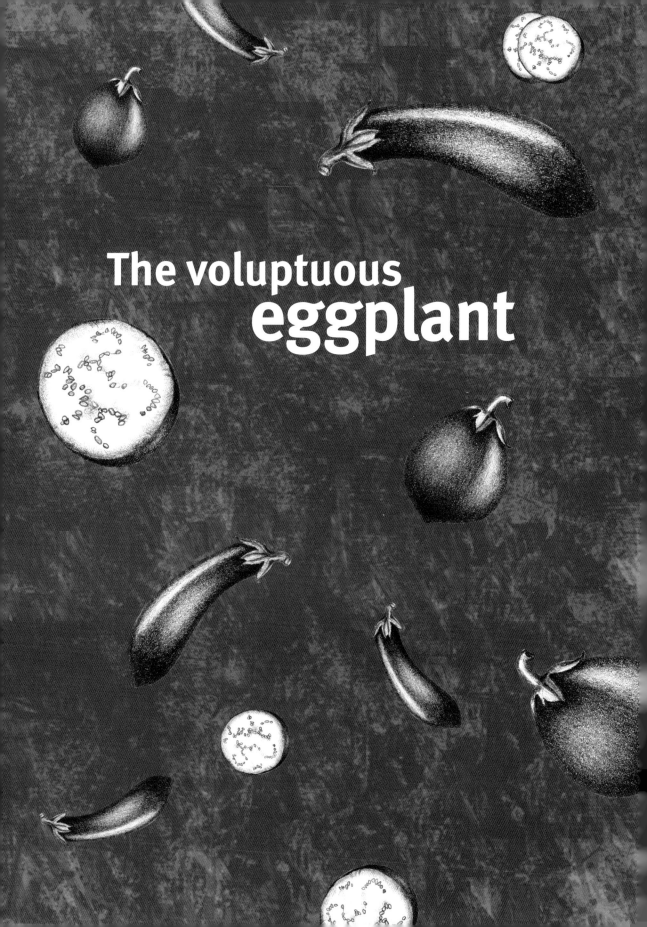

The voluptuous
eggplant

The voluptuous eggplant

For me, this seductive, sensuous vegetable is pure delight. It does not matter if you call it aubergine or brinjal, melanzane or eggplant. It does not matter if it is large, small, oval, long. I am happy to eat eggplant in any form—baked, grilled, marinated, in a sauce, as baingan bharta or baba ghanoush. Whatever, however and wherever, eggplant always does the trick for me.

The eggplant is a member of the nightshade family closely related to the tomato, and just like its red, juicy cousin, it, too, was at one time considered poisonous. In fact, the Italian word for it, melanzana, is said to come from the Latin mela insana, or poisonous (literally unhealthy) apple. Melanzane is also said to have aphrodisiac properties, and in India it was considered a forbidden vegetable, especially for priests. This could very well explain my penchant for it.

Italians use a lot of eggplant, especially in their antipasti and pastas. The eggplant isn't native to Europe though, but to India, from where it travelled to Italy with the Arabs during the Middle Ages. Since then, the Italians have been throwing them in just about every dish imaginable, always with delicious results. Every mama has her own special recipe for eggplant, and every region has their own melanzane speciality—the stuffed eggplant from Liguria, the coteletta di melanzane from Lazio, caponata, the moreish dip from Sicily. If you like this vegetable, you will never starve in Italy.

Here are a few of my favourite recipes. I bet you too will be seduced right away, even if so far you have been a bit suspicious of these vixen veggies.

> Be careful how you choose an eggplant. The skin should be smooth, without any bruises, and the lighter, the better. The heavier ones have more seeds in them, which means more bitterness.

Insalata di riso con melanzane

Eggplant & rice salad | Sicily

Yet another Sicilian masterpiece, this rice salad features capers, which give it a nice, sharp edge. In fact, in this chapter most of the recipes are from Sicily, as eggplant can easily be called the Sicilian national vegetable!

200 g boiled Basmati rice, cooked, drained and slightly cooled
400 g eggplant
1 tbsp capers, washed
1 handful mint
2 tbsp olive oil
Oil for frying
Salt & pepper to season

1 Peel the eggplant and cut it into cubes. Sprinkle with salt and let it stand so all the bitterness is drained away, say 30 minutes. Rinse and pat dry with paper towels.

2 Heat the oil and fry the eggplant till golden in colour.

3 In a bowl, combine the rice, fried eggplant, mint, olive oil and capers. Season with salt and pepper. Serve at room temperature.

> You could add some cherry tomato or normal tomato if you want to add some colour. Also add some chopped black olive.

Melanzane al forno con insalata e pomodoro

Baked eggplant with salad & cherry tomatoes | Diva classic

This is a dish I like to do when I don't want to go shopping, as it's made from the most basic ingredients of the Italian bhandar. It looks great, tastes even better and works as a starter, as a vegetarian main course for lunch, or just as part of a large buffet.

500 g round, large eggplant
2 tbsp dried oregano
1 handful fresh mint
100 g cherry tomatoes, halved
4 cloves garlic, finely chopped
2 limes, squeezed
A few tbsp extra virgin olive oil
1 handful rocket leaves or any salad leaf, washed and torn

1 Preheat oven to 200°C.

2 Slice the eggplant into ½-inch thick discs. Sprinkle with salt, and leave for 30 minutes to draw out the bitter juices. Rinse and pat dry with paper towels.

3 Line a baking tray with foil, and brush with olive oil. Sprinkle salt, pepper, oregano, mint and garlic on the foil. Place the aubergine slices on the foil, brush the tops with olive oil, and sprinkle again with oregano and garlic.

4 Bake for about 20 minutes, turn the slices over and bake for a few more minutes.

5 Wash and dry the salad leaves.

6 Transfer the eggplant to a serving platter and season with salt and pepper. Top it up with salad leaves and cherry tomatoes. Squeeze some lime juice on it and drizzle it with some more virgin olive oil.

> This is a light and healthy option. You could always add some Parmesan shavings to it if you like.

Frittelle di melanzane

Eggplant & goat's cheese fritters | Veneto

These fritters are dangerous because once you start eating them, there is no stopping. I normally like to make these as little bite-sized balls for cocktail parties, or as snacks at larger dinners. You could also fry them in the shape of little burgers as a starter.

3 large eggplants
1 handful parsley, chopped
2 tbsp flour, sifted
2 tbsp course bread crumbs
50 g Parmesan
1 small onion, finely chopped
1 egg, lightly beaten
100 g goat's cheese
Salt & pepper to season

1 Preheat oven to 250°C.

2 Bake the eggplants whole, till the skin bursts. Or you could do it the old fashioned way like I do, which is to cook them over a naked flame, on the stove, as for baingan bharta, till the skin is charred.

3 Let the eggplants cool, peel off the skin and scoop out the pulp. Make sure you remove the seedy part. It's always better to use just the white flesh.

4 Mash the flesh with a fork, add the parsley, both cheeses, the egg, chopped onion and enough bread crumbs for the mixture to bind together. The consistency should be of loose dough. Season with salt and crushed pepper. Chill the mixture for at least an hour.

5 Dust your palms with a little bit of flour, and shape the dough in small balls. Roll each ball in flour, shake off any excess and fry in very hot oil. Serve right away. The frittelle lose their crispiness very quickly.

Melanzane alla Parmigiana

Eggplant Parmesan | Naples

I first ate this famous Neapolitan dish in a plush restaurant in New York, doused with sweetish tomato sauce, way too much mozzarella and not a trace of Parmesan. Of course I hated it. Fortunately, later, I tried many delightful versions. One of the most delicate and memorable ones I've had was at San Lorenzo, a venerable Italian restaurant in London. It is one of their classics and, I believe, still on its menu after decades.

750 g eggplant
500 g basic tomato sauce (p 27)
250 g fresh mozzarella, sliced
50 ml olive oil
1 handful basil
100 g Parmesan, grated
½ tsp butter
Salt
Sifted flour for dusting

1 Slice the eggplant into rounds, sprinkle with salt and set aside for 30 minutes to draw out the bitterness. Rinse and pat dry with paper towels.

2 Preheat oven to 200°C.

3 Rinse the eggplant slices in cold water, then pat dry with paper towels. Lightly flour each slice. Heat 4 – 5 tbsp of olive oil and fry the eggplant slices on both sides until golden and soft. Season with salt. Continue until all the eggplant is cooked.

4 Grease a baking dish lightly with oil, and arrange alternate layers of tomato sauce, eggplant slices, both cheeses and whole basil leaves until all the ingredients are used up, beginning with tomato sauce and ending with Parmesan. Dot with butter, cover with aluminium foil, place in the oven and bake for about 20 minutes.

5 Remove the foil and continue baking 10 minutes longer to brown the cheese. Serve hot.

> This dish tastes nice the following day too, served at room temperature. I love to use leftover melanzane alla Parmigiana as a sandwich filling for lunch. It is yummy, yummy, yummy!

Melanzane ripiene

Stuffed eggplant | Liguria

A dish from the northwest coast of Italy, this Ligurian eggplant is surprisingly delicious—even for those who do not think of a baingan main course as particularly delicious. I used to do this as a vegetarian main course in MezzaLuna, and till date people ask us to prepare it for them at Diva.

8 small eggplants, the size
  of your hand or smaller
100 g bread crumbs
100 g Parmesan, grated
1 handful cubed Provolone
  or mozzarella
2 eggs
3 tbsp boiled rice
1 large clove garlic, minced
1 handful basil, chopped
Salt to taste
Oil for frying

1 Wash and dry the eggplants and cut each in half, lengthwise. Scoop out the flesh from each piece, being careful not to come too close to the skin. Leave about one eighth inch of flesh attached to the skin.

2 Boil the skins for about 5 minutes until just tender, and then transfer to a strainer.

3 Meanwhile, chop the eggplant flesh into very small pieces, and fry till golden. Place the bread crumbs, cheese, eggs, garlic, basil, rice and salt in a mixing bowl, with the fried eggplant flesh, and mix well. Taste a little bit of the mix to check that the seasoning, especially salt, is to your taste.

4 Now take the boiled eggplant shells and poke each gently with a fork in a few places. My Italian friend Ferda used to say this is done so that the eggplants don't explode while frying. Lightly salt the eggplant shells and fill them with the mixture; spread out the filling a bit to be sure it reaches all ends of the shell. Also, tuck a cube or 2 of mozzarella into the stuffing of each eggplant. You want to place the filling such that it is fairly level with the shell, but a little domed on the top.

5 Now you're ready to fry the shells. Heat about an inch of oil in a shallow pan. When hot, put the eggplants in, stuffing side up. Fry for about 5 minutes or until golden brown. Flip, and then fry the other side for a few minutes as well. Remove and drain on paper towels.

> I sometimes prefer to bake these, instead of frying. After I have stuffed the eggplant shells, I bake them in a preheated oven (200°C) for about 20 minutes. You could also add some minced meat or crumbled sausages to the stuffing. I like to eat this dish as it is, but you could serve it with some basic tomato sauce (p 27).

Penne alla Norma

Penne with eggplant | Sicily

This pasta features in all menus in Sicily. It is simple, delicious and with the addition of toasted ricotta, turns into an elegant and unusual dish.

1 packet penne
½ kg eggplant, cubed
  and fried
300 g basic tomato sauce
  (p 27)
50 ml olive oil
1 whole dried chilli,
  broken in two
100 g ricotta (optional)

1 Prepare the penne (p 5).

2 Heat the olive oil in a pan and fry the chilli for about 4 – 5 minutes, then remove the chilli from the oil.

3 Add the basic tomato sauce and the fried eggplant to the oil. Add the cooked penne with some of its cooking water to the sauce and toss well.

4 Now you have two options. You can either serve it as it is—or you grill the ricotta in oven, for about 4 – 5 minutes, till it turns slightly brown, and use that as a topping to the pasta. In Taormina, a wonderful seaside resort on the east coast of Sicily, they use ricotta salata, a hardened cheese, but since that is not available, I make it with fresh ricotta, and it works pretty well.

> When you are adding the sauce to the pasta it is always a good idea to save some sauce for topping. It gives the pasta more body as well as colour.

Melanzane sott'olio

Preserved eggplant | Sicily

Think of this as an Italian achaar.

2 kg large round eggplant
50 ml white wine vinegar
400 ml olive oil
3 – 4 dried red chillies, broken
3 garlic cloves minced
2 tbsp dried oregano
Salt to season

1 Cut the eggplants into one eighth inch juliennes. Sprinkle with salt and set aside for about 30 minutes to draw out the bitterness. Put the eggplant juliennes in a piece of muslin and squeeze them to draw out the bitter juices. Now place a lid on top of the eggplant juliennes and weigh it down with some heavy weight. The idea is to get all natural water out of the vegetable. Set aside, weighted down, for 24 hours.

2 Drain all the liquid, put the eggplant juliennes in a clean muslin cloth, and squeeze again. Place in a bowl and sprinkle some oil. Add the chilli, garlic and oregano and mix well. Spoon the mixture into sterilised airtight containers, pressing the mixture in tightly to get rid of any air pockets. Cover with oil, seal and store.

Anna, my dear Sicilian friend at whose cooking school I learnt to love Sicilian food (more on that in the next chapter), says eggplant sott'olio should be preserved for a minimum of 2 months, but I never have that much patience. I always divide the mixture into smaller jars, so that I can start eating some after a couple of weeks. It is not as sharp, but still very nice.

Caponata alla Loredana

Eggplant relish alla Loredana | Naples

This is another recipe from gorgeous Loredana. At one of her parties she made this version of caponata and it was so fantastic that the next day we had introduced it on the Italian Cultural Centre menu as caponata alla Loredana. I have replicated the recipe exactly the way she narrated it to me. I have also included the classic recipe after this one. You can choose which one you prefer.

4 eggplants
4 red peppers
1 onion
1 celery
1 carrot
2 squares of chocolate
  with 70% cocoa content
½ cup vinegar
2 spoons sugar
1 fistful pine seeds
1 fistful raisins
1 fistful almonds, peeled
  and cut
Salt & pepper to season
Oil for frying

1 Cut the eggplants in cubes and leave in lightly salted water for 15 minutes. Wash, dry and deep fry.

2 Cut the peppers in cubes and fry.

3 In a frying pan, brown the sugar with a spoon of water, add the chocolate and carrot, onion and celery, all minced. Mix for 2 minutes with 2 spoons of olive oil and add almonds, raisins, pine seeds, salt and pepper.

4 Mix well and finally add the eggplants and peppers, then the vinegar, and let it cook on a slow fire for 15 minutes. Store in a sealed container and enjoy after 3 days.

Classic caponata

Classic eggplant relish | Sicily

Like with most Sicilian classics, here too you can see the heavy Arab influence—north Africa is after all just across the sea. This is the traditional recipe for caponata, but again it varies from region to region. You could add fish, squid, artichokes or even octopus to it. However, I like my caponata simple, with just eggplant, or Loredana's variation with peppers. Use this as a topping for crostini, eat it cold as a salad, or even serve it as a side dish with fish.

1 kg eggplant
1 large onion, diced
1 stalk celery, diced
2 tbsp sugar
150 ml tomato purée
2 tbsp capers, washed
2 tbsp green olives, pitted
  and chopped
100 ml white wine vinegar
100 ml olive oil
1 tbsp dark cocoa powder or
  grated dark chocolate

1 Cut the eggplants in cubes and leave in lightly salted water for 15 minutes. Wash, dry and deep-fry.

2 In a pan, add half of the olive oil and the onions. Make sure you add the onion while the oil is still cold. Let it cook on a slow fire till soft, around 5 minutes, and set the onions aside.

3 In the same pan, repeat the process with the celery, cooking on a slow flame. Set the celery aside.

4 Now cook the tomato purée with vinegar, sugar and cocoa powder and season with salt and pepper, say about 10 minutes.

5 In a large mixing bowl, gently incorporate the eggplant, celery, onion, capers and olives in the tomato mixture. The tomato purée should just cover the vegetables and not be very liquid. Store in an airtight container and serve the following day.

Purea di melanzane

Purée of roasted eggplant | Sicily

When I tasted this dish for the first time as part of a large antipasti buffet, it seemed like a cross between baingan bharta and the Lebanese baba ghanoush, accenting again the strong Arab influence in Sicilian food. You could eat this dish as a starter served with some grilled bruschetta, as part of a cocktail menu, or just as a side dish. The mellow flavour of roasted garlic works beautifully with that of well-roasted eggplant.

1 large eggplant
1 whole head of garlic, papery
  outer layers removed
50 ml extra virgin olive oil
Juice of 1 lime
2 tbsp cream (optional)
1 handful parsley, chopped
Salt & pepper to season

1 Preheat oven to 220°C.

2 Poke the eggplant skin in several places. Place the whole head of garlic on a baking sheet with the eggplant and roast in a baking dish in the oven until the flesh is very tender, about 45 – 60 minutes. If the outer layers of the garlic begin to brown before the eggplant is tender, remove it from the oven.

3 When the eggplant is cool enough to handle, break it open and scoop the flesh out into a mixing bowl. If the eggplant has too much seed, remove some of the black seedy part.

4 Separate the garlic into individual cloves and squeeze the pulp into the eggplant. Add the oil, and give the purée a good whisk until smooth. Stir in the chopped parsley. Add cream if you like, and serve at room temperature.

> When I don't want to add cream I just add a good squeeze of lime, which makes it lighter and more refreshing.

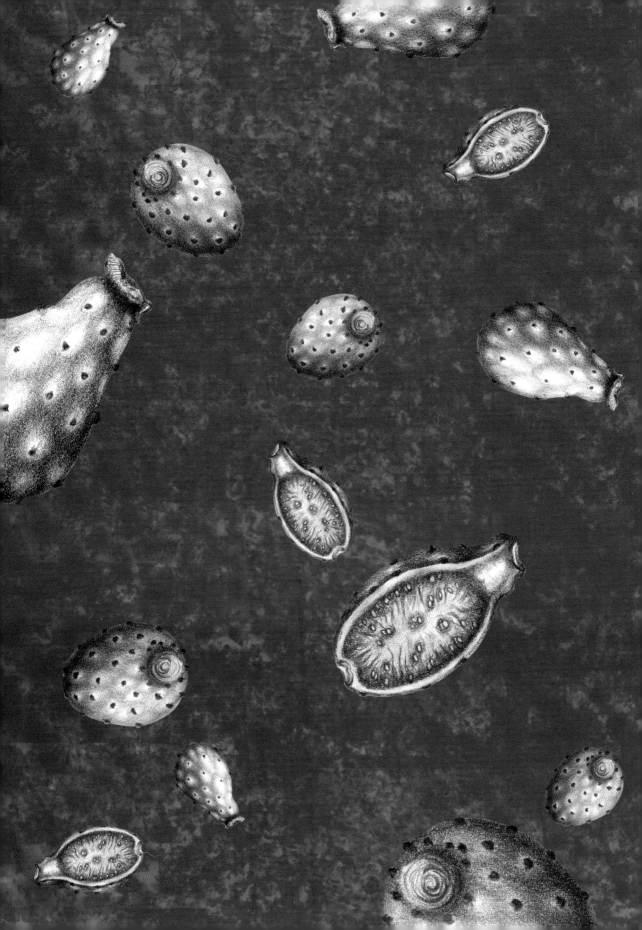

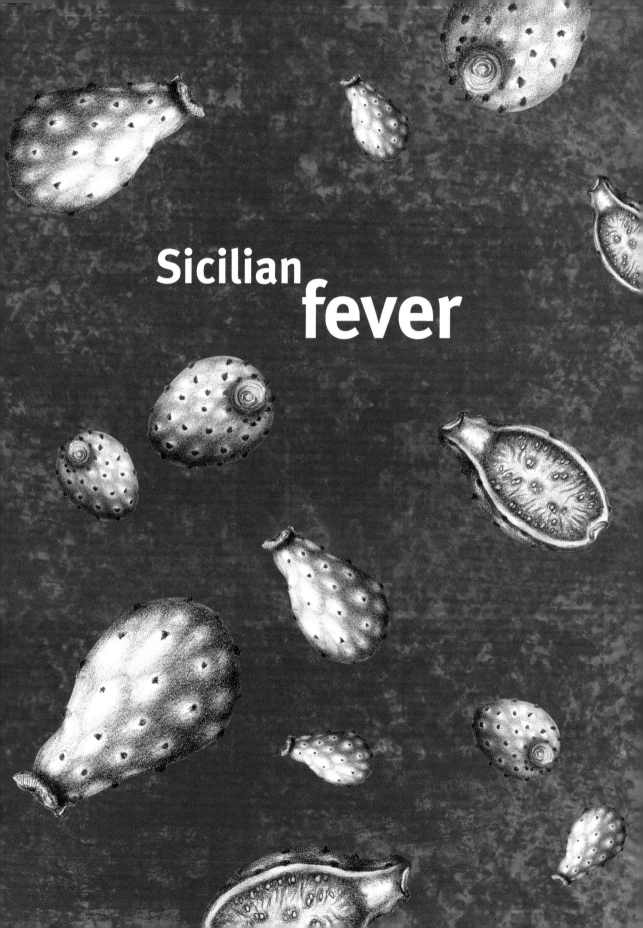

Sicilian fever

Sicilian fever

I did not want to arrange this book by region or course, but here is an exception. Sicily is very close to my heart. For me, it really is a special part of Italy, so much so that I have often considered spending a part of my life there.

I discovered Sicily through a book. I was in Los Angeles visiting my younger sister who was studying at university there. While she was attending her classes I would browse through all the book and music shops near the campus. During one such leisurely afternoon, I stumbled across *The Heart of Sicily: Recipes and Reminiscences of Regaleali,* written by Marchessa Anna Tasca Lanza. I flipped through the book and knew I had to have it. As the title suggested, it was just not a cookbook—the author shared her world with me, told me about the land and life in the Sicilian countryside, of the passing of seasons, of the saints' days and birthdays, of the yearly harvest and the daily milking. Her enthusiasm for the food of Sicily was contagious. She made me want to run to the kitchen and cook. At the same time, I was reading Giuseppe di Lampedusa's novel, *The Leopard,* and was deeply impressed by Lampedusa's loving descriptions of Sicilian food. What was it about Sicily and food? I had to find out.

The cover of Lanza's book said that the marchessa ran a cooking school and that the family also had their own vineyard. MezzaLuna was in its first year then, and by the time I returned to Delhi, I was determined to find out a bit more about this tiny Sicilian village called Regaleali, not even marked on my atlas. In those days we didn't have Google to rely on, so I called my friend Serra, who lived in the town of Lerici in the Italian Riviera, and asked her to do some investigating for me.

Three days later, Serra had the phone number of the Tasca D'Almerita winery.

I had just returned from America and couldn't really afford another trip abroad but I could not resist. I decided to call immediately.

On the phone, Anna sounded rather stern and grandmotherly. I explained to her while trying not to sound absolutely crazy, that I loved her book and wanted to attend her cooking school right away. The next session, I learnt, started in September, a month later. The duration of the course was a week. I think she was a bit shocked when I told her that I would like to stay longer, until I thought I had learnt all that they could teach me. Furious fax messages were exchanged the next few weeks, and all the arrangements were made. I would get there in the second week of September, start the course solo, and other students would join the week after. Serra too decided to treat herself to a 3-day course, and was to join me later along with the other students.

I arrived at Palermo and was met by Anna's sister, Costanza, who drove me to Regaleali with her after lunch. Costanza appeared extremely serious and aloof and I, usually a chatterbox, found myself mute with discomfort all through the drive. It was only later, once I had gotten to know her better, that I realised the aloofness was a shield for her shyness. Through the drive I alternated between excitement and nervousness. Would I be a good enough student? Would they be disappointed? Would I be disappointed? The drive was beautiful, particularly once we got to Regaleali. The hillsides were green with vines. As we approached Casa Vecchia, Anna's home, we passed through miles and miles of tomatoes kissing the Sicilian sun, and fields of plump grapes, ready to be plucked. The earth and grass was sun-baked and golden. I fell in love with Casa Vecchia—with its peeling blue doors, stone walls and terracotta roof—the minute we pulled into the driveway. This was to be my home in the coming weeks.

Anna must have been around sixty at that time and I liked her immediately. Dinner that night was with her parents, the Count and Comtessa Tasca D'Almerita, who made me feel at home right away. They were all very curious about me—a strange young Indian girl who had landed in this tiny world of theirs. It was the time of the grape harvest, the vendemmia, and emotions were running high, as it was a risky period, a time of enormous gamble.

Count Tasca, who even at eighty was a romantic at heart, became my favourite. He produced a wine called Nozze D'Oro for his wife, with the most heartfelt note inscribed on the label, for their 50th wedding anniversary. His constant question to me was, 'When will you cook me an Indian meal,' and I kept my promise and cooked him a meal of aloo puri, bhindi and bharta before I left. I kept in touch with him through letters and postcards for many years till he died five years ago.

Next morning, I was summoned at 6 am. The day began with milking the sheep to make ricotta. The next lesson was bread making. A huge wood-fired oven was lit up in Anna's large, cozy kitchen, and suddenly 10 kilos of flour were placed in front of me. The secret to making good Sicilian bread, I was informed, was the punching of the dough. The longer and stronger the punching, the better the bread would be. I still smile when I think about me trying to compete with Carmello, Regaleali's baker for the last 30 years, punching 10 kilos of dough with all my might. Of course, I was no match for him, and my arms ached for the next two days.

During the afternoon we marinated and preserved vegetables for the antipasti. The scales of economy worked very well at Regaleali. They ate only what they grew and raised themselves. The poultry and meat were raised on the grounds. Anna's vegetable and herb garden was dotted with large purple eggplants, vivid red and yellow peppers competing with the fall flowers and heavy tomatoes hanging from near-withered plants. Cheese was made from sheep's milk. All the produce was used.

The next seven days passed quickly between learning to make Costanza's risotto, Aunt Salina's timballo, Anna's cassata Siciliana, and delicious arancine rice balls stuffed with beef ragu. I made ricotta, plucked blood oranges for the salad and for marinating prawns, and prickly pears and quince for jams and marmalades. They were long, tiring and exhilarating days.

Dinner conversations were always animated with arguments and debates over recipes, history and whether or not the bridge between Sicily and the rest of Italy should be demolished. The only problem was that I was getting hungrier and hungrier with every passing day. In those days I was still a vegetarian and the pastas were normally made with meat and fish, so my dinner would consist of the vegetables served with the second course and salad. I don't think anyone noticed and I was too shy to mention it. But wine was always flowing in abundance, which made up for my empty stomach.

Then the students arrived. Ince from Turkey, Anthony Bay from England, Emma from Paris, Beppe from Milano, Olga from New York and my friend Serra from Liguria. I was already Anna's self-appointed assistant by then, and had everybody's respect. I might have been the youngest, but had been there longer than any of them.

That night I saw a frown on Serra's face when she saw me eat my dinner. The next morning we went to Erice to visit and work with Maria Grammatico at her famous pastry store. A runaway from a convent, she specialised in convent sweets. All of us watched wide-eyed and open-mouthed as her expert hands made pasta reale, moulding and painting these sweets made of marzipan. Apples, bunches of grapes, every imaginable fruit and vegetable was moulded from the marzipan dough.

Serra informed Anna that we would not be eating lunch with the group, but would join them later. I was kidnapped and taken to a nice trattoria nearby, where Serra rapidly ordered food. I did not understand a word, just that a lot was coming! Then began the investigation. Had I been eating salad all these days? Had I not told them I was a vegetarian? Had nobody noticed my empty dinner plate?

That lunch was pure gluttony. She had ordered a full vegetarian meal, selection of antipasti, couscous (an important staple of Sicily), penne alla norma, risotto con carciofi, sfincione (Sicilian pizza), followed by canollo, which remains my favorite Sicilian dessert to this day. I had been cooking furiously for the last few days. Now for the first time I also tasted what the Sicilian kitchen was all about. Serra had a conversation with Anna that evening (yes, Serra can be slightly aggressive), and from that day on, a portion of pasta was always saved for me before the meat or fish was added to it.

What with learning various desserts, pesce spada, panelle, caponata, pesto with a twist (Sicilians add tomatoes to it), it was already the last day. All of us had to start preparing, early in the morning, for the gala dinner. Of course, when the menu was decided, Anna was careful to add a few vegetarian things for me.

That night, after a very merry and drunken meal, we sat in the courtyard talking till the night grew faint. That autumn has stayed with me ever since. It was not simply about learning to cook the Sicilian cuisine—those weeks gave me a real taste of rural Sicilian living. For many years I thought of living in Sicily for a few months every year. Until recently we even planned to buy a small cottage somewhere in a tiny village until we were dissuaded by more practical friends.

Although I have returned to Regaleali, after Anna converted part of Casa Vecchia into a guesthouse, my first experience could never be repeated. I was no longer a young, enthusiastic student, ready to imbibe everything.

And oh yes, before I forget, there was a connection between Lampedusa's *The Leopard* and Regaleali. Count Tasca was known as the 'last of the leopards'.

Arancine
Stuffed rice balls

Arancia in Italian means oranges, and these delicious rice croquettes are called little oranges, perhaps because of their shape and crisp, golden appearance. Miniature versions of these work well as finger food for a big party, medium-sized as part of a fritto misto—a mixed plate of fried food, usually vegetables cooked in batter—or regular-sized as great antipasti. Traditionally the filling is made with minced beef. I have used minced mutton instead.

FOR THE FILLING
400 g minced mutton
75 ml olive oil
1 medium onion, finely chopped
2 tbsp celery, chopped
½ tsp chilli flakes
75 g frozen, shelled peas
200 g basic tomato sauce (p 27)
½ kg basic risotto (p 6)
2 eggs, beaten

1 Brown the minced meat well in a saucepan set over a high flame, and set aside.

2 In another pan, heat the olive oil and sauté all vegetables till golden brown. Add the tomato sauce, peas and the fried mince. Cook the filling on very low heat for about 30 – 40 minutes. Let it cool completely, then refrigerate so that it can be as dry as possible when you make the arancine.

3 Prepare the basic risotto, and when it is still slightly warm, add the beaten eggs.

4 For assembling the arancine: take the filling out of the fridge, some bread crumbs in a bowl and the risotto. Wet your hands, and shape some rice into a ball in your cupped hand. Make a well in the centre of the ball, in which you place a spoonful of filling, then fold the rice over to seal the ball.

5 Roll the ball in bread crumbs and set it aside. Repeat this till all the rice is used up.

6 Fry the balls in very hot oil till crisp and golden.

> Anna says the filling—ragoncino—should always be prepared a day in advance so that the meat can soak in all the flavours. I do a vegetarian version, replacing the minced meat with vegetables like carrots, zucchini and celery. You can play with the filling as imaginatively as you like.

Panelle
Chickpea chips

I just adore panelle. When I ate these for the first time in the sleepy little Sicilian town of Erice, I was amazed at their similarity to paapri. However, once I learnt how to make them, I realised a slightly different technique was used. Panelle are easy to make, and I normally serve them in paper cones at large parties. They make great drink time snacks.

200 ml water
200 g chickpea flour
Salt & pepper to season
Oil for frying

1 Pour the water into a saucepan and add the chickpea flour, whisking the mix continuously to ensure that no lumps form. Season with salt and pepper.

2 Cook the batter over medium heat, stirring constantly, for say 5 minutes till it gets the consistency of a thick béchamel. Remove from heat.

3 Now you have to be very quick with your hands. Using a flexible spatula, spread the dough onto a flat surface like the back of a baking sheet. It should form a sheet not more than ¼ of an inch thick.

4 Allow the dough to cool. Once cool, loosen the edges with a flat knife and peel it off. Cut into triangles, or if you feel like having some fun, just do crazy slashes and make whatever shape you want.

5 Heat the oil, and fry the chips in medium heat, not too many at a time. They should be golden and slightly puffed (remember paapri!). Serve right away.

Zucchine all'aceto sott'olio
Preserved zucchini

The first lesson at Anna's cooking school was preserving vegetables, which could then be used as part of antipasti or for a summer lunch with warm bread and some cold cuts. Let's call it the Sicilian achaar. Using this method, you can make it with any kind of squash such as golden pumpkin, zucchini, and of course, eggplant (eggplant sott'olio, p 166). For years zucchine all'aceto sott'olio was part of my antipasti buffet at MezzaLuna, and I still make it at home.

2 kg zucchini, cut into long,
 1/8-inch thick juliennes
50 ml white wine vinegar
400 ml olive oil
3 – 4 dried red chillies, broken
3 garlic cloves minced
2 tbsp dried oregano
Salt to taste

1 Place the zucchini juliennes in a large bowl and sprinkle with salt and vinegar. Place a lid on top of the juliennes and weigh the lid down with some heavy weight. The idea is to force all the natural water out of the vegetable. Set aside the juliennes under the weight, for 24 hours.

2 Drain all the liquid, put the juliennes in a clean muslin cloth, and give them a final squeeze.

3 Place in a bowl and sprinkle some oil over it. Add the chilli, garlic and oregano and mix well. Spoon the mixture into sterilised airtight containers, pressing the mixture in tightly to prevent air pockets. Cover with oil, seal and store.

> Anna says the sott'olio should be preserved for a minimum of 2 months, but I never have that much patience. I always divide the mixture in smaller jars, so that I can start eating after 3 or 4 weeks. It is not as sharp, but still very nice.

Frittata al forno
Baked frittata

I like frittatas because they make great snacks, light lunches and even a perfect picnic meal. They give a regular omelette a whole new dimension all together. This recipe is from Anna's second book, *The Flavors of Sicily*, however I have modified it to my taste.

500 g ripe tomatoes
1 medium onion,
  thinly sliced
1 medium red bell
  pepper, sliced
6 eggs
1 handful basil
2 tbsp bread crumbs
50 g grated Pecorino
  or Parmesan
50 g Gruyère
Salt & sugar
1 tsp fuoco sauce (p 145)

1 Remove the seeds from the tomatoes and cut them into cubes. Place the cubed tomato in a colander and sprinkle with salt and sugar. Let it drain for about 20 minutes.

2 Blanch the onion and pepper in salted boiling water for a minute, and remove from the fire. Drain and pat dry.

3 Preheat oven to 180°C.

4 Grease a baking tin with olive oil. Sprinkle the bottom and sides with bread crumbs.

5 Squeeze the water out of the tomatoes, onions and pepper. In a mixing bowl, beat the egg yolk with tomatoes, onion, pepper, both the cheeses and basil. Season with salt. Add the fuoco sauce.

6 Beat the egg white till it forms peaks and fold in gently with the yolk mixture.

7 Pour into the baking tray and bake for about 20 – 25 minutes. The frittata will rise like a soufflé and then fall as it cools. Serve warm or at room temperature.

Pasta con il pesto al pomodoro
Pasta with tomato pesto

In Sicily, they add tomatoes to pesto, and eat it with pasta and thinly sliced potatoes. We ate this dish for the first time on a holiday in the east coast of Sicily. This pesto also goes very well with fish, as a sauce for dipping bread, or even as a spread for bruschetta.

2 bunches basil
1 bunch parsley
2 cloves garlic, peeled
50 g Pecorino cheese, grated,
  if not available, use Parmesan
50 g pine nuts
100 g tomatoes, skinned
  and deseeded
100 ml olive oil
Salt & pepper to season
1 large potato, peeled and
  thinly sliced
1 packet any long pasta,
  such as spaghetti, linguine
  or tagliolini

1 Blend all the ingredients, except the pasta and potatoes, in a food processor. Of course, if you are a romantic and want to make the pesto in the traditional way, grind all the ingredients into a rough paste with a pestle and mortar.

2 Cook the pasta and potato in salted water till the former is al dente. Drain the pasta, reserving a little of the water in which it was cooked. The potatoes should be very thinly sliced so that they cook fast.

3 Toss the pasta and potatoes with enough pesto to coat well, adding a little pasta water to give it a nice consistency. Spoon some more pesto on top before serving.

> Any leftover pesto can be kept in the fridge for 4 – 5 days. Of course if you freeze it, it will last forever.

Timbaletti di Salina
Aunty Salina's filled pasta timbales

These pretty moulds—pasta shells filled with ham and melting cheeses—are an all time favourite of mine and many Diva regulars. First featured in the MezzaLuna menu, they're still requested for at Diva. Aunty Salina was very considerate. Though she prepared it in a large family-size mould, she taught me to make smaller ones so that I could adapt it to individual portions at the restaurant.

1 packet angel hair pasta, or very thin spaghetti
Béchamel sauce, made from 50 g butter, 4 tbsp flour and 200 ml milk (p 25)
150 g any mixed cheeses, but one has to be a melty cheese, and definitely some Parmesan
100 g cooked ham, cut in small cubes
A few bread crumbs
Salt & pepper

1 First make the béchamel sauce.

2 Preheat oven to 250°C.

3 Take a large mould or smaller individual moulds, and grease them well with butter. Dust the bottom and sides of the mould with bread crumbs and set aside.

4 Cook the pasta till al dente in salted water, and quickly toss it in half of the béchamel sauce. In a separate mixing bowl, add the cheese and ham to the remaining béchamel.

5 To assemble, line the bottom and sides of the mould with most of the pasta, to form a shell shape. Fill the shell with the ham and cheese mixture. Cover the mixture with the remaining pasta, pressing it down gently. Dot with butter and dust with some more bread crumbs.

6 Bake in the oven for at least 45 minutes, till the crust is golden. Let it set for 15 minutes, then serve it warm.

> You need to use moulds which are circular and deep. Another good filling for the timbale is the ragoncino meat filling for arancine (p 177). I also do a vegetarian version, where instead of ham I use sautéed mushrooms or steamed, tender asparagus. Smaller versions can be breaded and fried, larger versions can be baked in the oven.

Pesce al forno
Baked fish with herbs & capers

This classic fish recipe from Sicily calls for swordfish. However in Delhi I make it with kingfish, which is also a good fish for cutting in steaks. You are bound to find it in every trattoria and restaurant on the Sicilian coast.

600 g kingfish, or any firm-fleshed fish that can be cut into 1 inch thick steaks
1 onion, thickly sliced
2 cloves garlic, sliced
1 tsp dried rosemary
1 tbsp dried oregano
1 handful mint
25 g butter
25 ml olive oil
75 ml any white wine
Salt & pepper to season

FOR THE SAUCE
50 ml red wine vinegar
½ tsp sugar
Juice of 2 limes
30 ml olive oil
1 clove garlic, minced
1 handful parsley, chopped
1 handful capers, rinsed
Salt & pepper to season

1 Preheat oven to 150°C, for about 10 minutes.

2 Lightly grease a shallow baking dish and place the fish steaks in it.

3 Surround the fish with the sliced onion and garlic. Sprinkle with all the herbs, salt and pepper. Dot with bits of butter and drops of olive oil. Bake for about 5 minutes.

4 Add the wine and bake again till the fish is done, or another 5 minutes. Normally 10 minutes is the total amount of time taken in the oven.

5 While the fish is baking, quickly make the sauce. In a small bowl, mix the vinegar and sugar, add all the other ingredients and give it all a nice whisk.

6 When the fish is done, transfer it to a serving plate, spoon the pan juices on top, and finally add a bit of the sauce.

Spezzatino di agnello
Lamb stew

I first ate this simple lamb stew at the home of some friends in Palermo and thought it was out of this world. When I asked the lady of the manor for the recipe, she was quite perplexed. All she had done was throw the leftover vegetables in. So really, this stew is about using whatever you have at hand in your veggie basket.

1 kg boneless lamb, cubed
2 onions, roughly chopped
200 g potatoes, preferably
  the old variety
100 g carrot, cut into chunks
2 stalks celery, chopped
200 g tomatoes, blanched,
  peeled and roughly chopped
1 large eggplant, peeled and
  cut in cubes
100 g bell pepper, chopped
75 ml white wine
1 handful mint
300 ml brown stock or
  vegetable stock
1 tbsp flour

1 Cook the onion in a heavy saucepan. Add the lamb and brown the pieces on a high flame for 2 minutes.

2 In another large pot, layer the vegetables and meat, starting with a meat and onion layer at the bottom, and alternating with vegetables. Season each layer with salt and pepper. Add the stock, white wine, tomato purée and mint leaves, saving a few sprigs for the garnish. Bring to a boil, reduce the heat and cook, covered, until the meat is tender, for about two hours.

3 Mix the flour into a cup of water to make a watery mix. Add this into the sauce to give it a glaze and thicken the sauce. Cook for another few minutes. Garnish with mint, and serve with mashed potatoes or crusty bread.

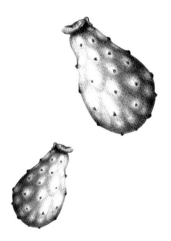

Biscotti regina
The queen's cookies

I absolutely adore these cookies, and not just because they taste so good. They have helped save my skin many times. When MezzaLuna had just opened, Gita asked me if I catered. Being a good Marwari girl, I was not going to let any business get away. So I said yes. I was desperate, the restaurant was always empty, and pay day was not too far away. Of course we messed it up big time. The following day, Gita came, insisting that she pay me in full, and asked a single question, 'This was your first catering job, wasn't it?' I nearly died of shame. The following day, I sent her a large jar of biscotti regina, with a heartfelt note. I was forgiven. Gita says it was my note, but I know it was these wonderful cookies. I like to call them 'forgive me' cookies. This recipe comes from Anna's book, *The Heart of Sicily*.

5 cups flour
1 cup sugar
220 g butter, cubed
1 large egg
4 eggs, separated
½ cup water
2 cups white sesame seeds
1 pinch salt

1 Place the flour, salt and sugar on a clean work surface or in a big mixing bowl, and mix well. Work the butter into the flour, until the mixture is crumbly. Make a well in the centre and add in the whole egg and the egg yolks. Blend together and knead well till the dough is soft. Wrap it in cling film and refrigerate for at least 30 minutes.

2 Divide the dough into 6 – 7 pieces, and roll each piece into a long rope, about an inch thick. Cut the ropes into 1 inch long pieces.

3 Preheat oven to 200°C. Line a baking tray with foil or parchment paper.

4 Lightly beat the egg whites in a bowl with a fork, adding water. Place the sesame seeds in another bowl.

5 Now we are ready to rock! Drop the biscotti pieces first in the egg white mix, 15 – 20 pieces at a time, then lift them and transfer to the bowl with the sesame seeds, shaking well, so that the biscotti are evenly coated with sesame.

6 Form each biscotti into an olive shape, pressing the sesame seeds into the dough. Place the biscotti on the baking sheet and bake for about 30 minutes, till brown.

7 Turn off the oven, leaving the biscotti in for another 5 minutes. Cool and store in airtight containers.

Cannoli
Pastry tubes with ricotta cream

Every Sicilian man believes making a cannolo is a man's job. It is hard work, rolling out the cannolo, so papa has to do it and mama can never match his skills. (Mind you, I have yet to see a Sicilian man actually do anything in the kitchen.) Every time I have a largish party or I have to set a buffet, I make cannoli so, so small that they just vanish into your mouth. But for a sit-down dinner I recommend making slightly larger shells.

FOR THE SHELLS
150 g flour
50 g butter
1 tsp vinegar
100 ml (approx) water
1 egg white, slightly beaten
Oil for frying

FOR THE CREMA DI RICOTTA
(RICOTTA CREAM)
300 g ricotta
75 g sugar
2 tbsp candied orange peel
  or candied fruit, chopped

1 First make the crema di ricotta. Drain the ricotta of any liquid and refrigerate it overnight. Blend in the food processor till smooth.

2 Place the ricotta in a mixing bowl, add sugar and beat with a whisk or hand-held electrical whisk, till light and fluffy. Add in the chopped candied fruit and place the crema in the fridge.

3 Next, make the shells. Mix together the flour and butter, add vinegar and then slowly add just enough water for the dough to hold together, approximately 100 ml. You need to make a stiff dough here, and not a soft, elastic one.

4 Dust a surface with some flour and start rolling out the dough, till it is quite thin. Cut out discs of dough with a round cutter, or use a large steel katori.

cont. on next page >

5 Now you need a metal tube or bamboo stick with a diameter of about an inch. Roll each disc around the tube such that it takes the shape of a hollow tube.

6 Deep fry the cannoli in hot oil till golden and crisp, while it is still on the stick. Keep plenty of kitchen towels ready to slide the fried cannoli off the tube, since it's going to be very hot. Set aside. Fry all the discs like this, then allow them to cool.

7 Fill each with ricotta cream before serving. Dust with icing sugar and decorate with candied fruit, if desired.

> Ricotta cream is very handy, as it can be used in many desserts: eaten by itself with a splash of honey, stuffed in choux pastry, or even served with fruits.

> Cannoli tubes can be stored in airtight containers for many days, so don't worry if you make some extra. They will be used sooner or later. My friend Massimo, who produces marsala wine, told me that he uses marsala instead of vinegar in the dough. I too have tried it with wine, and it does work very well, indeed.

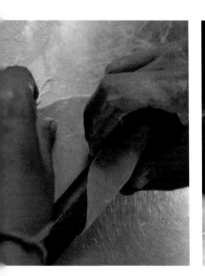

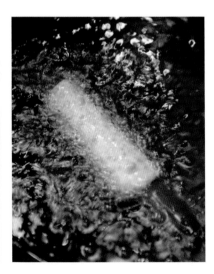

Nectar of the gods

Nectar of the
gods

Wine is regarded as a necessary accompaniment to food by Italians. Every region has its own gems and sometimes, to a visitor, the entire country seems like a vast vineyard. I was once told by an Italian that each region produces wines which will complement the food from the area, and he would never dream of drinking a wine from Alto Adige with his Sicilian meal. I am not, fortunately, that fussy.

Wines are primarily labelled in two ways: either for the grape it is made with or the region where it's made. New world wines tend to label their bottles with the grape variety and the wine maker. For example, Joseph Phelps, Cabernet Sauvignon, 1997. French wines label their wines by the region and sometimes the winemaker but never by the grape. So, Chateaux Margaux, 1997 or Puligny Montrachet, Etienne Sauzet, 1997.

Italian wines tend to be more complex, and are labelled both by grape name and by region. Here is a very brief introduction to the major Italian wines, both red and white. Most of the major white wines in Italy come from the Fruili region, while most of the major reds come from Piedmont. I feel that the Italian reds are, in general, stronger than Italian whites—but wine, like food, is all about individual tastes and this is very much a personal bias. I would ask you to try as many varieties as you can before you form your opinion.

White wine

Pinot Grigio

Probably the most well known Italian white wine, Pinot Grigio is the Italian name for the grape Pinot Gris. This light, dry wine, produced in Veneto, has a subtle, lemony, nutty flavour and comes in a wide price range. Pinot Grigio goes well with simply cooked, light food: grilled fish, salads, and seafood.

Orvieto

Located in Umbria, central Italy, Orvieto is named after a village near where it is produced. It is a dry wine made from Trebbiano and Grechetto grapes. Umbria's warmer climate gives this wine an earthiness which you will not find in wines from the Piedmont or Veneto region. This wine is made in the same way since the Romans began to make it. I would drink it with grilled chicken or fish.

Soave

Soave is a close cousin to Pinot Grigio. Also grown in Veneto, Soave is a light, straw-coloured, slightly sweet, fruity wine. It is made from Trebbiano and Garganega grapes and is best consumed young. I would drink it with a light salad, or maybe an asparagus tart.

Gavi

Gavi is a very dry, delicate wine with pronounced acidity. It is named after the town of Gavi in Piedmont, in the northwest of Italy. Produced from local Cortese grapes, it has delicate and complex aromas of grapefruit, honey, and flowers. I would happily drink it with avocado mousse.

Arneis

Arneis means 'rascal' in its local Italian dialect, and is also a product of Piedmont. Light and easy to drink, Arneis is a great summer drink, suited particularly to salads and light pastas. Arneis is very refreshing, and also works as an aperitif or pre-dinner drink. Named after the grape from which the wine is made, Arneis is a medium dry wine with a rich texture and hints of peaches, apricots, and pears.

Chardonnay

Chardonnay is the king of white wine grapes, capable of a complexity and delicacy that is unsurpassed. Italy also makes great Chardonnay. Most Italian Chardonnay is made in the Alto Adige region in the mountainous north. Recently, even Sicily has started producing great Chardonnays. In general, Italian Chardonnays are far crisper and less 'deep' tasting than their New World or French counterparts. You could have it as an aperitif, or with seafood pasta, or just some marinated prawns.

Red wine

Barolo

Barolo is one of the world's greatest red wines and my all-time favourite. It is big, powerful and full-bodied with a complex mixture of tastes and textures. Like most of the heavy wines of Piedmont, it is made with Nebbiolo grapes. Barolo gets better and better with age, and is a wine I recommend you drink and lay away for the future. I love a good Barolo so much that I tend to drink it on its own, maybe nibble on a piece of Parmesan with it. I feel the same with Brunello—though I should mention here, sometimes I like to make a risotto with good Barolo and potatoes.

Chianti

Chianti is perhaps Italy's best known red wine. It comes from Tuscany and is named after the region where it is made. It has come a long way from its cheap and cheerful days, when it was a wicker wrapped bottle, ordered with a plate of pasta in a humble trattoria. Today you can see more well crafted, expensive versions in the market and Chiantis of varying price ranges. It is traditionally eaten with a pizza or a pasta or a simple meal.

Barbaresco

Barbaresco is Barolo's near neighbour and stylistic soulmate. It is also produced from Nebbiolo grapes, but tends to be softer and slightly more graceful. It complements the rich heavy food of Piedmont very well. It would complement a roast, or a pasta with heavy sauce, or just a plate of cheese.

Bardolino

Bardolino is a light, fruit-filled wine made in the Veneto region of Italy. Named after the town of Bardolino on Lake Garda, this wine has faint cherry flavours and just a hint of spiciness. A blend of many grapes including Corvina, Molinara and Rondinella, it is sometimes made into a dry, rose, sparkling wine called Chiaretto. Bardolino is best served chilled. It goes nicely with seafood, light meats, pizzas and pastas.

Amarone di Valpolicella

Crafted, primarily from Corvina grapes, this wonderful red is from the Veneto region. It is a fairly heavy wine and best drunk with red meats, robust sauces, or if you are like me, with more or less everything. I even like to use it in my cooking if someone is willing to pay for it.

Brunello di Montalcino

Montalcino is Tuscany's second most famous wine zone, after Chianti. In terms of quality, however, it is the shining star. Brunello means 'the nice, dark one' in local dialect. It is Tuscany's most expensive and rare wine. By Italian law, Brunello must be aged longer than any other wine—a minimum of four years. Brunello di Montalcino is created entirely from Sangiovese grapes. No mixing, no fusion here. It truly is a pristine wine.

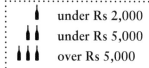

▮	under Rs 2,000
▮▮	under Rs 5,000
▮▮▮	over Rs 5,000

The greatest thing about Italian wines is that they provide the best value for their taste. A young wine enthusiast will find far better variety and bargains among Italian wines than among any other wines from around the world. Today most of my favorite Italian wines are listed in restaurants and hotels all over the country.

The wines listed below, I am happy to drink always. Although some of them might be above your range, maybe you can treat yourself to them on a special occasion. They're worth it!

Reds

▮▮▮ Amarone di Valpolicella, Masi, Veneto

▮▮▮ Barolo Casetta, Piedmont

▮▮▮ Masetto, Tenuta dell'Ornellia, Toscana

▮▮ Mille e un notte, Donna Fugata, Sicily

▮▮ Primitivo, Tormaresca, Puglia

▮▮ Rosso Del Conte, Tasca D'Almerita, Sicily

▮▮▮ Sassicaia, Bolgheri Sassicaia, Toscana

▮▮▮ Sori San Lorenzo, Angelo Gaja, Piedmont

▮▮▮ Tignanello, Villa Antinori, Toscana

Whites

▮▮ Capo Martino IGT, Jermann, Venezia

▮▮▮ Gavi di gavi, Marchessi Di Barolo, Piedmont

▮▮ Nozzo D'oro, Tasca D'Almerita, Sicily

▮ Prosecco Moletto Spumante, Veneto

▮▮▮ Ross Bassj, Angelo Gaja, Piedmont

▮▮▮ Sauvignon Sanct Valentin DOC, St Michael Eppan, Alto Adige

▮▮▮ Were Dreams, IGT Jermann Venezia

A bit of bubbly now

My niece recently introduced me to a young singer called Colbie Caillat who has a great song called 'Bubbly'. The words go something like, 'It starts in my toes, makes me crinkle my nose'. Well that's exactly what a glass of good Prosecco does to me.

Prosecco is an Italian sparkling white, made in the Veneto region with Prosecco grapes, with an addition of Pinot Grigio grapes. It is lemony, light, refreshing and dry. Originally it was supposed to be a white wine with a slight fizz, but today it is a proper sparkling wine. Prosecco is the traditional base for the famous Bellini from Harry's Bar in Venice, and is great drunk on its own as an aperitif (an opening drink before your meal), or mixed with fresh fruit juices as a cocktail.

Something stronger, maybe?

Italians do not like to waste anything. So with the pomace (seeds), stalks and stems of the grapes they produce a very unique by product called grappa. This Italian brandy has 40–45 percent alcohol content and although delicious, is very potent and—beware—extremely strong.

Traditionally, grappa is served chilled in small glasses, after the meal, as a digestif. Grappa should be swirled gently in the glass and then brought to your nose, before tasting. It is then drunk in small sips. In Italy, grappa is also added to espresso to make a caffe correto, a popular after dinner concoction.

Menus

Menus

The Italians take their meal times very seriously, and a meal normally consists of antipasti, which literally means 'before the meal' or a starter; followed by a primo or the first course, which would be either a pasta, or rice or a soup; followed by secondi, a second course of meat or fish. Of course dessert and cheese follow, but they are not of prime importance. A piece of fruit will suffice. In recent years, Italians too have become health conscious and you might find them skipping a course during lunch. On the other hand if you go to the countryside, you will find yet another course, I piatti di mezzo, or the middle course, of salad and a small flan—in between the pasta and the main course. All this is downed with loads of local wine.

In today's world, where we are all so pressed for time, the Italian style of eating comes as a respite. Of course sometimes it is difficult to go through so many courses so you can play around with the basic format. I have listed some menus for you, but by the time you are done with this book, I bet you will be creating your own fabulous menus.

Buon Appetito!

Eating by yourself

Option 1
Tomato basil bruschetta, and a hearty minestrone

Option 2
A huge plate of Caesar salad—a meal by itself

Option 3
Simple grilled fish with green salad

Option 4
Spaghetti olio aglio

Option 5
Spaghetti puttanesca and then a fruit salad to cool down

TV Dinners

Tray 1
Lamb stew and a glass of red wine, maybe

Tray 2
Penne with cauliflower and an insalata caprese

Tray 3
Baked frittata, purée of roasted eggplant with some veggie sticks

Alfresco meals

Barbecue with friends
Beetroot and berry shots
Marinated grilled vegetables
Bruschetta with caponata
Chicken with mascarpone
Tiramisu

Lazy outdoor lunch
(starts as brunch and continues till high tea)
Crusty bread with fuoco sauce
Lasagne with meat sauce
Eggplant & rice salad
Preserved zucchini
Ciambella di mele

Picnic hamper

Hamper 1
Breadsticks with fuoco sauce
Baked frittata
Rice & spinach tart
Caponata
Marinated grilled vegetables
Chocolate salame

Hamper 2
Marinated prawns
Eggs with tarragon
Stuffed eggplant
Panzanella
Mushroom flan
Torta di ricotta

Sit-down dinners

Showing off | summer
Starter Marinated prawns or carrot flan
First course Zucchini carbonara or spaghetti puttanesca
Main course Sabrina's saltimbocca
Dessert Chocolate torta

Showing off | winter
Starter Polenta alla griglia
First course Risotto with pumpkin & bacon
Main course Pork roulade
Dessert Torta della nonna

Informal easy dinner with friends | summer
Starter Ela's Caesar salad
First course Pasta with kingfish
Dessert Italian fruit salad

Informal easy dinner with friends | winter
Starter Bruschetta with caponata
First course Pumpkin soup
Main course Lamb with egg & lemon sauce
Dessert Tiramisu

In the mood for love

An elegant, light supper
Starter Avocado mousse
First course Linguine with vodka & caviar
Main course Fish in a citrus marinade
Dessert Pana cotta with mangoes

Only aphrodisiacs
Starter Asparagus tart, small
First course Spaghetti with seafood in a paper parcel
Main course Warm lobster salad (serve as main course)
Dessert Strawberries with red wine & mascarpone

Dinner for a date
(early days of romance, you are playing the kitchen god/goddess here!)

Aperitif Prosecco or flute of champagne with dates wrapped in bacon, whilst you chit chat on the couch
Starter Marinated artichoke salad
Main course Pork fillet with capers
Dessert Chocolate cake

Kitchen goddess 2
Aperitif Champagne with bite-size polenta
Starter Braised figs with Parma ham
First course Gnocchi with Gorgonzola
Main course Chicken with sesame
Dessert Peaches poached in wine

Though this is a wholesome dinner, we have cut out the first course—food is important, but there might be other things on your agenda here.

The big night

Canapés 1
Bagna cauda

Arancine

Panelle

Crostini with fuoco sauce

Eggplant & goat cheese fritters

Bruschetta with tomato & basil

Baby cannolo

Canapés 2
Frittata with Gorgonzola

Dates wrapped in bacon

Polenta squares with mushroom

Mozzarella in carozza

Bite-sized chocolate torta

Baby cannolo

Buffet
Ela's Caesar salad

Braised figs with Parma ham

Grilled vegetable platter

Insalata caprese

Penne alla Norma

Lasagne with pesto & potatoes

Roast leg of lamb

Strawberries with mascarpone

Torta della nonna

Bake the chocolate torta in a square or rectangle baking tray, and then cut the cake into neat 2 inch squares.

The grand feast

Panzanella

Roasted onion with Parmesan

Preserved eggplant

Spaghetti puttanesca

Lasagne with meat sauce

Mushroom flan

Fish with citrus marinade

Whole chicken with pomegranate

Peaches poached in wine

Chocolate salame

Last minute guests

(dinner in under an hour)

Option 1

First course Spaghetti aglio olio or mozzarella carrozza

Main course Pollo alla diavola

Dessert Italian fruit salad

Option 2

First course Penne with cauliflower or Insalata caprese

Main course Paula's Fish

Dessert Strawberry in red wine

Option 3

First course Panzanella

Main course Pollo alla valdostana

Dessert Apple ring cake

For vegetarians

Sit-down dinner 1
Starter Eggplant & goat cheese fritters
First course Minestrone
Main course Filo pie with spinach, ricotta & mushroom

Sit-down dinner 2
Starter Mozzarella in carozza
First course Penne alla Norma
Main course Grilled polenta

Buffet
Avocado mousse

Panzanella

Insalata caprese

Melanzane alla Parmigiana

Rice & spinach tart

Lasagne with potato & pesto

Asparagus tart

Chocolate torta

Strawberry with mascarpone

Taste in
words

Taste in
words

I like food, I like books, and I like books about food. I don't mean just cookbooks, but novels, anthologies, travelogues, memoirs. Anything as long as it contains many delicious thoughts of food.

This is a list of my favourite books on food, the books that have made eating and cooking even more special for me.

Like Water for Chocolate Laura Esquivel

I have read Laura Esquivel's book—a heady combination of love, romance and tragedy all emoted through food, and set in Mexico—many times over, tasting every recipe and feeling every emotion of the protagonist, Tita. How can one not be seduced by passages like: 'The strange alchemical phenomenon seemed to have occurred, not only Tita's blood but her whole being had dissolved into the rose sauce, into the quail, and into every aroma of the meal, that's how she invaded Pedro's body, voluptuously, ardently fragrant and utterly sensual.'

Aphrodite Isabel Allende

What can better the pleasure of your favourite author writing about your favourite subject. I have read every one of Isabel Allende's books, but *Aphrodite* was a sheer delight from cover to cover. I even had an event at Diva based on the book, which was a great success. Every recipe and method was followed religiously, including dabbing truffle oil behind my ears when making the 're-conciliation soup'.

Comfort Me with Apples Ruth Reichl

I first read *Tender at the Bone,* the first helping of celebrated food writer, Ruth Reichl's memoir, followed by *Comfort Me with Apples.* It is all about her adventures with food and sex. The title of the book comes from the Song of Solomon, 'Comfort me with apples, for I am sick with love'.

Kitchen Confidential Anthony Bourdain

Despite being a chef, I have to admit Anthony Bourdain's first book is an absolute riot. I even went to eat at his restaurant Brasserie Les Halles in New York after reading the book, only to be disappointed. But that still does not change how entertainingly he has described the frenzy, the buzz and the frantic high pressure of a restaurant kitchen. This is what he writes about women line cooks: 'One woman, Sharon managed to hold down a busy sauté station while seven months pregnant, and still find time to hand out advice to the unhappy broiler man. A long time associate Beth who likes to refer to herself as a 'grill bitch', excelled at putting fools and loudmouths into their proper place. She refused to behave any different than her male co-workers. I have been fortunate to work with these studly women. No weak reeds here.'

Al Dente: The Adventures of a Gastronome in Italy William Black

When I read William Black's book, I felt he was writing on my behalf, for he had done what I have always dreamt of doing—spending two years of 'blissful investigation', tracing and savouring all that the Italian kitchen had to offer. Interspersed with simple recipes, this is a must for any lover of Italian food.

....

I also have a list of my favourite Italian cookbooks. The only problem is that they are not easy to get hold of. However, thanks to Amazon, and online ordering, this is not an impossible task. These are a few 'musts' in my opinion. Even after all these years, I still like to browse through them once in a while.

The River Café Cook Book Ruth Rogers and Rose Grey

River Café Cook Book Easy Ruth Rogers and Rose Grey

Tuscany: The Beautiful Cookbook Lorenza De'Medici

The Heart of Sicily: Recipes and Reminiscences of Regaleali Anna Tasca Lanza

Flavours of Sicily Anna Tasca Lanza

Bitter Almonds Mary Taylor Simeti

The Essentials of Classical Italian Cooking
Marcella Hazan
(My editor swears by this book, and I had to order it as soon as I heard her describe Hazan's recipe for a roast chicken stuffed with lemons.)

A night at the cinema

When I was a kid, I had a secret desire to eat roast chicken, because I loved the way it looked in Tom and Jerry cartoons. That's the power animation has. It turned a good Marwari vegetarian girl into a carnivore. That was a long time ago, but even today when I hear the sizzle of batter dropping into hot oil, or see prawns turn pink on the big screen, I feel like making a beeline for the kitchen. Here is my list of movies to watch when you have food on your mind.

Babette's Feast

Now, this is a feast I would like to recreate—the full monty with the wines and champagne—as soon as I win the lottery.

Like Water for Chocolate

Very few films can do justice to the book on which they are based. This is one film which may be as good, if not better, than the book. Beware! You will be very hungry and very, very amorous after watching it.

Mostly Martha

This is a brilliant German film about an idiosyncratic, obsessive chef called Martha. I remember one line from the film particularly, when she is preparing some salmon: 'A chef can be judged by the simplicity of his ingredients. In this recipe there is nothing to distract you, no design, no exotic ingredients and there is only fish and the sauce'.

Eat Drink Man Woman

This is a film made by Ang Lee in the 1990s when he was still making movies in Asia. It is about a great chef who is losing his tastebuds. Every Sunday he whips up a feast for his three daughters, who really don't care too much for the food. I adored the film and also saw the western remake, *Tortilla Soup*, which was nice but not a patch on the original. I have never seen food displayed or prepared in a movie as well as it was here.

Big Night

How can I write an Italian cookbook and talk about food movies and not include *Big Night*? It's a very funny film about two Italian American brothers who try to save their ailing Italian restaurant in New Jersey. When you watch it, you'll almost smell the basil and taste the melting cheese.

Woman on Top

Penelope Cruz has never been more lovely than in this film, especially in the scene when she bites into a piece of red chilli. This movie is also about love, food and sensuality. It's worth watching just for Penelope.

List of suppliers

List of suppliers

Delhi

Allied Fruits & Plants
Shop No 58 B, Khan Market
(011) 24642509 | 24619310 | 41757003

Prunes, dates, olives, caper, pasta, olive oil, balsamic vinegar, lady finger biscuits, filo pastry sheets, fruits, vegetables, fresh and dry herbs

Big Bazaar
Sahara Mall, Sector 28, Gurgaon
(0124) 4008888

Pasta, olive oil, dry herbs, balsamic vinegar and Arborio rice, fresh vegetables available

Bombay Fruit Mart
54A Khan Market
(011) 24617729 | 24655865 | 25260790

All types of Italian cheeses including Parmesan, Gorgonzola and Provolone

Namdhari's Fresh
S1/A, Arjun Nagar, Safdarjung Enclave
Near Kamal Cinema, New Delhi
(011) 65646881 | (0) 9911745676

Fresh herbs, all vegetables and fruits

Kishen and Sons
Yashwant Place Market, Chanakyapuri
(011) 24671895

One stop shop for Italian cheeses, Arborio rice, olive oil, pasta, pork sausages and filo pastry

Le Marche
58 Basant Lok, Priya Complex,
Vasant Vihar
(011) 41669111

Sg 104 DLF Galleria, DLF City Phase IV,
Gurgaon 122001
(0124) 2806131

Colavita oil, pastas, cheese, balsamic vinegar, Flander's Dairy products, lady finger biscuits for tiramisu, olives, capers, sun-dried tomatoes, polenta

Lucky Stores
Shop No 120, INA Market
(011) 24624550

Arborio rice, all types of pasta, balsamic vinegar, seasonings, canned tomatoes, polenta, filo pastry, Italian cheeses, dry herbs

PigPo
9 Jorbagh Market
(011) 24611723 | 24626930

5 Shanti Niketan Market
(011) 24115335

All pork products, also mutton and chicken

Steak House
Jorbagh Market, New Delhi
(011) 24611008/ 1129 | 24658034

All types of Italian cheeses, Parma ham, salami, bacon, mortadella and other pork products

Store 18 Super Market
K2 Somdutt Tower, Sector 18, Noida
Noida 210 301
(0120) 2516931 | 2516932

One stop shop for all types of Italian
cheeses, pasta, olive oil, vinegar, canned
and bottled products, vegetables and
fresh herbs

Mumbai

Godrej Nature's Basket
Shop No 2-7, Ground Floor, Samrat
Vaibhav, Opp Tarapore Towers, Andheri
(022) 26300766/ 7

30A Arcade, Gate No 4, WTC,
Cuffe Parade
(022) 22154706 | 40028006

Most Italian cheeses, ham, salami, bacon,
and other pork products

Indigo Deli
Ground Floor, Feroze Building
Chatrapati Shivaji Maharishi Marg
Apollo Bunder
(022) 67305316 | 66551010

Cold cuts, cheeses, balsamic vinegars, olive
oils, wine

Rajat Provision Store
20 Mt Pleasant Road, Off Napeancy Road
Rajat Apartment, Malabar Hill
(022) 23637707

Pastas, olive oil, balsamic vinegar, olives,
capers, mustard, all dry goods and canned
products.

Roman Store
C. Green Building, Shop No 4 & 5,
Bank of Maharashtra Lane,
Versova, Andheri (W)
(022) 2634 1652 | 2633 8317

Shop No 5, Vireshwar Prakash, Opp. Mu-
nicipality Office, Nehru Road, Villa Parla
(022) 26143318

Colavita olive oil, cheeses, cold cuts, dry
goods, olives, capers, balsamic vinegar.

Also, you will find all types of vegetables,
fruits, herbs at the wholesale Crawford
Market.

Chennai

Maison des Gourmets
5, Cenotaph Road, 2nd Lane Alwarpet
(044) 64502050/ 40

All Italian cheese, pork products, ham

Nilgiri Dairy Farm
103, Dr Radha Krishnan Street, Mylapore
(044) 28110321

One stop shop for all types of Italian
cheeses, cold cuts, meat, dry goods, olive
oil, balsamic vinegar and canned goods

Nilgiris
#13/A, Velachery Main Road, Velachery
(near Sri Vasavi Mobiles)
(044) 22432730

#1, Shanmugam Apts, Mogappair
(044) 26560144/5

#321, Arcot Road, Vadapalani
(044) 23651577 | 23650657

Nilgiris Nest
#105, Dr. Radhakrishnan Road, Mylapore
(near A.V.M. Kalyana Mandapam)
(044) 28111772 | 28115111

Spencer's Daily
#100/A5, Ponnambalam Road,
K.K. Nagar (near Sivan Temple)
(044) 42616738/ 9

#370, Shop #5 & 6, Bypass Road,
Velachery (opp. IOB Bank)
(044) 42021630/ 27

#168 Chinna Krishna Tower,
MTH Road, Villavakkam
(044) 26182921

#22, Thanikachalam Road, T Nagar
(044) 42126218/ 36

All types of Italian cheeses, cold cuts, meat,
dry goods, olive oil, balsamic vinegar,
canned goods. They also have a vegetable
and fruit section with every vegetable and
herb that you might need.

Reliance Fresh
24 Raja Annamalai Road,
Puraswalkam Flowers Road
(044) 43539653

#19/4, Abhinav Centre, Co-operative
Colony, Charminar Road, Alwarpet
(044) 43009462

#7/3, Muthukrishnan Street,
Pondy Bazaar, T. Nagar
(044) 42125401

#456, 3rd Avenue, Indira Nagar, Adyar
(044) 42695861/2

#3721, Mullam Village, 6th Avenue,
Anna Nagar
(044) 42693052

Fresh herbs and vegetables, sausages,
cheese, pasta, olives, Colavita olive oil

Additionally, Koyambedu Market sells all
types of fruit, vegetables and fresh herbs.

Bangalore

Namdhari's Fresh
#134, Doopanahalli Road,
60 Feet Domlur Road, Indiranagar
(080) 251152909/ 10
indiranagar@namdharifresh.com
www.namdharifresh.com

#821, Kusal Arcade, 20th Main,
80 Feet Road, opp. National Games
Village, Koramangala
(080) 51103777/ 8
koramangala@namdharifresh.com

Olive oil, cheeses, vinegar, herbs, all fruits
and vegetables

Spencer's Super
2/1, 3 Mosque Road, Frazer Town
(080) 25807771/ 2

Site No. 8, Indiranagar,
80 Feet Main Road, HAL III Phase
(080) 25212966 / 1804 / 1805

#86, Spencer's Tower, 16th Cross,
R.T. Street, MG Road
(080) 41122244

Sunny's
Embassy Diamante, 34 Vittal Mallya Road
(080) 22243642 | 41329366/ 91 | 22120496
sunnysblr@yahoo.co.in

Variety of cheeses, processed meats, including smoked bacon, German sausages, Black
Forest ham

Thoms Bakery & Super Market
No.1/2, Wheelers Rd
Frazer Town
(080) 25301860 | 25361076

Colavita olive oil, Italian dry products

Calcutta

C3 The Market Place
Lee Residency, 26 Lee Road, Elgin Road
(033) 22834343

C3, City Centre
Shop #E-004, Dc-1, Sector 1, Salt Lake
Bidhan Nagar
(033) 23581118 | 23581242

One stop shop for all Italian products,
cheese, cold cuts, oils, vinegar etc

Sincerity Stores
3, Ground Floor, Lake Road
(033) 24630727/ 6 | 65261743

All Italian dry goods

Spencers
375, South City Mall, Prince Anwar Shah
Road, Jodhpur Park
(033) 44025536/ 7

369/4, Avishar Shopping Complex,
Nr E M Byepass, Purbachal Kalitala Road
(033) 24843746/ 7

Cereals, food grains, spices, dry fruits,
edible oils, sugar, salt and other groceries
all available at Burrabazar Market, MG
Road (near the flyover)—also, fresh fruits
and vegetables, fresh herbs, pasta, olive oil,
sausages, bacon, vinegar etc.

Vegetable Products Limited
No. 5 & 6 Fancy Lane, GPO
(near Vijaya Bank)
(033) 22100266

Fresh vegetables fruits and herbs

Jaipur

Dairy Craft (India) Pvt. Ltd.
A-33, Flat No 3, Raghav Apartment
Shyam Nagar
(0141) 2295087 | (0) 9928784777
dairycft@del13.vsnl.net.in

Indian mascarpone, ricotta, imported
Italian cheeses

Hi-growth Associates
573, Urmila Path, Vivek Vihar
Shyam Nagar Extension
(0141) 6451827 | (0) 9414159451
higrowth_udr@yahoo.com

All pork and meat products, cheeses

KL Enterprises
561, Natani Bhawan, Maniharon Ka Rasta
Tripolia Bazar
(0141) 2328259 | (0) 9829014324
natani_manish@rediffmail.com

All Italian dry goods—pasta, olive oil, dry
herbs, balsamic vinegar

Shri Krishna Trading Corporation
C-24, Jai Singh Highway, Bani Park
(0141) 4081175
enamtdg@yahoo.com

All Italian dry goods

The Right Connection
1, A.C. Market, Raja Park, Jaipur
(0) 9829077786 | (0) 9351383001
deepakorganic@yahoo.com

Vegetables, salad leaves and fresh herbs

Chandigarh

Empire Store
SCO No10, Sector 17-E
(near Neelam Theatre)
(0172) 2703440

All Italian dry goods

Rlcr Super Mkt
Scf-4, Sec-18c, Sector-18
(0172) 2544454 | 2774477

All Italian ingredients and cold cuts

Reliance Fresh
PH-5, Mohali
(0172) 5020774

Sector-22
(0172) 4604426

Sco-301-302, Sector-38 D
(0172) 4604434

Goa

Magsons Super Centre at Miramar
DB Road, Miramar
(0832) 2463700

All Italian dry goods plus pork products,
cheeses, fresh vegetables and herbs

Pune

Dorabjee
M G Road, Opp Kakade Mall, Pune Camp
(020) 26052882

Italian dry goods plus fresh herbs and
vegetables

Oberoi Hotels

Every Oberoi Hotel has a deli, Gourmet Shoppe, which stocks all pork products, Italian cheeses and cold cuts. www.oberoihotels.com.

Flanders Dairy

Flanders Dairy makes many Italian cheeses in India. They are stocked all over the country and also have their own website. www.flandersdairy.com

Metro Cash & Carry India

For the address of your local Metro Cash & Carry India in Bangalore, Hyderabad, Kolkata and Mumbai, visit www.metro.co.in. The stores stock all meats, cheeses, dry fruits, seafood, cold cuts, oils, vinegar and canned products.

Reliance Fresh

We've listed Reliance Fresh information for Chennai and Chandigarh. For your local Reliance Fresh store phone information and address in other cities, if you live in New Delhi, NCR (Ghaziabad, Noida, Faridabad and Gurgaon), Mumbai, Hyderabad, Jaipur or Pune, do refer to www.reliancefresh.info or email admin@reliancefresh.info.

All information correct at time of going to press.

Index

Index

A

Almonds
Caponata alla Loredana, 167
Torta della nonna, 112–13

Amaretti
Salame dolce, 59

Amaretto
Salame dolce, 59

Anchovies
Bagna cauda, 89
Spaghetti puttanesca, 148

Angel hair
Pasta con gremolata, 100
Timbaletti di Salina, 183

Apple
Ciambella alle mele, 83

Arborio rice
Risi e bisi, 50
Risotto al mare, 104
Risotto con barbabietola e
   formaggio di capra, 103
Torta di riso e spinaci, 51

Artichoke
Bagna cauda, 89
Insalata di carciofi marinati, 122

Asparagus
Torta di asparagi, 129

Avocado
Mousse di avocato, 121

B

Bacon
Arista di maiale, 154
Datteri con pancetta, 123
Pasta carbonara, 45
Penne alla Loredana, 49
Risotto di zucca con pancetta

croccante, 76
Tagliatelle al sugo di agnello, 48

Baguette
Bruschetta con pomodoro e basilico, 38
Insalata Cesare alla Ela, 68
Panzanella, 66

Baking powder
Torta della nonna, 112–13

Balsamic vinegar
Cipolle arrosto con Parmigiana, 95
Fragole con mascarpone, 138
Insalata di carciofi marinati, 122
Pana cotta, 139–40
Petti di pollo al balsamico, 108

Basil
Bruschetta con pomodoro e basilico, 38
Cosciotto di agnello alle erbe, 111
Frittata al forno, 181
Insalata caprese, 42
Insalata di arragosta, 133
Insalata di carciofi marinati, 122
Melanzane alla Parmigiana, 163
Minestrone di verdure, 40
Melanzane ripiene, 164
Panzanella, 66
Pasta alla kingfish, 150
Pasta con il pesto al pomodoro, 182
Pasta con pesto, 44
Pasta con pomodoro e basilico, 47
Pesto, 26
Petti di pollo al balsamico, 108
Pollo arrosto con melograno, 109
Sicilian fuoco, 145
Spaghetti al cartoccio, 127

Basmati rice
Insalata di riso con melanzane, 159

Béchamel
Béchamel sauce, 25
Crespelle con funghi, 93

O

P

Acknowledgements

This book is not a solo effort, and there are some very special people I need to thank:

Gorgeous Chiki Sarkar, my wonderful editor for keeping me on my toes—my dear, I did not know I could write a cookbook!

Sephi Bergerson, your wonderful photographs made me fall in love all over again—with my food and my hands!

My dearest Gita, for always indulging me and humouring me, without you there would be no Diva, and without Diva there would be no me.

Serra, my buddyji; without her brutal honesty I would still be cooking American-Italian food. Serra, now my ravioli does not taste as if it has come out of a can.

Simi, Shivani and Shefali: my wonderful friends from school, thank you for letting me experiment on you, and for suffering a spaghetti olio aglio when all you wanted to eat was chowmein, for waiting tables at MezzaLuna, for eating leftovers, and for always believing that I was a 'Bond'.

Ela: for always being so interested. For reading patiently whatever I wrote.

Aditya, my brother for letting me cook for you and even paying me for it. Thank you very much for the commercial enlightenment.

Siya, the bestest niece in the world, your inputs in the chapter 'Cooking for your beloved' was highly appreciated; you do have a fertile mind!

Lesley, you I need to thank in bold capital letters, THANK YOU. For staying up all those nights and correcting all my Ps and Qs so that I could meet the self imposed deadline. You are a real dude!

My star team, Ritu Gujral, Premchand, Naval, Niju, Rajesh, Dinesh, and each and every person in the Diva team, all of you rock! I know, I know, I have a terrible temper but you know that I love you.

All my guests at Diva, Le Café and the Italian Cultural Centre, thank you for being demanding and generous and ensuring that I keep experimenting! Without your regular patronage, boredom would have set in long time ago.